How to Get Rid of "it"

Before "it" Gets Rid of You

Topical Handbook for Healing and Deliverance from Negatives Attitudes

A Practical Self-Help Guide to Spiritual and Personal Growth

A series of easy spiritual exercises, interactive tools,
And step-by-step instructions to receive
Freedom from bondage
And experience spiritual healing and deliverance

Volume Six

ISBN-13: 978-1986308731

ISBN-10: 1986308731

How to Get Rid of "it"

Before "it" Gets Rid of You

Topical Handbook for Healing and Deliverance from Negatives Attitudes

A Practical Self-Help Guide to Spiritual and Personal Growth

A series of easy spiritual exercises, interactive tools,
And step-by-step instructions to receive
Freedom from bondage
And experience spiritual healing and deliverance

Volume Six

Compilations of Works
By
Dr. Paulette Douglas

DEDICATION
This book is dedicated to my Loving, Supportive, Faithful Sisters,
Mary Jane Woods Fields, Prenilla Ann Woods Lewis and Muriel Gail Woods

**My Sisters have always inspired me to be the Women that God has ordained me to be and
to continue to minister to God's people and to make full proof of my ministry**

CONTENT

How to Get Rid of "it", Before "it" Gets Rid of You

PREFACE

How to Get Rid of "it", Before "it" Gets Rid of You is a Deliverance and Spiritual Warfare Manual compiled by Dr. Paulette Douglas which is worth reading and re-reading more than once, in order to empower the reader when confronting personal crisis and trials. Dr. Paulette Douglas has compiled many practical, spiritual books bringing light to the evil that exists. She brings the deliverance ministry to the forefront, explaining how each and every believer can counteract evil and the devil. Not many believers understand the concept of the Holy Spirit and that we are all called to fight against the devil, our enemy. Dr. Paulette Douglas presents scriptural background and Bible passages from the old and new testaments, as well as prayers to share with the reader that each of us is called to resist and fight against the devil with the power of the Holy Spirit. Dr. Paulette Douglas refers to this as the deliverance ministry and explains this is one of the privileges all believers have at our disposal.

This background scripture material is necessary as many readers may be unfamiliar with these spiritual concepts. The main focus on the book is to be a manual; or one stop guide to show the reader what the bible has to say about deliverance as well as to expose the works and deceptions of the devil as well. The cover itself might seem an actual handbook- yet this book is truly a manual for deliverance. This exhaustive book contains too much information to be digested in a single, quick reading. The words contained are life changing. While some traditional readers and those in organized religion may find this book difficult to believe and a bit theatrical, a close-minded attitude is exactly what the devil wants in order to operate.

It is important to keep in mind the charismatic background of Dr. Paulette Douglas is based on the belief of the real workings of the Holy Spirit and the literal belief in modern day spiritual gifts such as tongues and healing. Much of the book is an invaluable resource where Dr. Douglas has taken scriptural truths and prayers and relates them to the modern-day believer to use and apply when facing any trial or work from the enemy. The scriptural references will empower any reader with a quick resource of how to respond in faith to any difficulty- large and small. It is a spiritual self-help book in the fact that it will allow the reader the tools to look within himself/her-self and identify any areas or issues where Satan has his foothold. Not only that it tells the reader how to face and address these issues! For those who are at a loss of how to begin to approach their spiritual problems there are a number of sample prayers applicable to any number of situations. The reader will get the impression as if this book was written for his or her own situation. This is a book to meditate on and use- and is not intended to collect dust on a book shelf. There are eleven sequels to this handbook which address many other issues that just might cover your "it".

In this twelve-book series, How to Get Rid of "it" Before "it" gets Rid of You we discuss evil spirits and how they operate:
1. The Apostolic anointing and ministry
2. How demons enter and oppress people
3. Curses and how to deal with them

4. Breaking bondages
5. Casting out spirits
6. Healing the wounded heart
7. Ungodly beliefs
8. Ministering to people
9. House cleansing
10. Discerning of spirits

In this volume we deal with the root causes of the "it' of negative attitudes and How to get rid of the "it" of negative attitudes before it gets rid of you. Negative attitudes are something what plagues many people today, whether negative attitudes to food, sex, drugs, alcohol, smoking, spending, masturbation, porn, etc. Some inexperienced deliverance ministers might go after a spirit of negative attitudes, which may bring freedom, but often, it doesn't bring lasting freedom. Many times, there is a root that needs to be pulled up, alongside casting out any residing spirits that are holding the person in bondage to the negative attitudes. Getting to the root of the negative attitudes is the key to bringing a person lasting genuine freedom. I am going to address the most common roots to negative attitudes, and hopefully give you an idea of how this bondage works so that you can minister lasting freedom to this type of bondage.

INTRODUCTION

"It Is Finished"
The Words of Victory

"When Jesus therefore had received the vinegar, he said, "It is finished.""—John 19:30
Words of triumph. In His words, "My God, my God, why hast thou forsaken me?" we heard the
Savior's cry of desolation. In His words, "I thirst" we listened to His cry of lamentation. Now
there falls upon our ears His cry of jubilation— "It is finished." From the words of the victim we
turn now to the words of the Victor. The Cross of Christ has two great sides to it: it showed the
profound depths of His humiliation, but it also marked the goal of the Incarnation, and further, it
told the consummation of His mission, and it forms the basis of our salvation.

It is finished." What is found in these three words, "It is finished" is wrapped up the Gospel of
God. In these words, contained the ground of the believer's assurance. In those words, is
discovered the sum of all joy, and the very spirit of all divine consolation. Every" it" that we
could ever encounter in our lives was dealt with on the cross therefore; we have the victory
through Jesus Christ over any and every "it".

"It is finished." This was not the despairing cry of a helpless martyr. It was not an expression of
satisfaction that the termination of His sufferings was now reached. It was not the last gasp of a
worn-out life. No, rather was it the declaration on the part of the divine Redeemer that all for
which He came from heaven to earth to do, was now done; that all that was needed to reveal the
full character of God had now been accomplished; that all that was required by the Law before
sinners could be saved, had now been performed—that the full price of our redemption was now
paid.

"It is finished." The great purpose of God in the history of man was now accomplished—from
the beginning, God's purpose has always been one and indivisible. It had been declared to men
in numerous ways: in symbol and type, by mysterious hints and by plain intimations, through
Messianic prediction and through didactic declaration. That purpose of God may be summarized
thus: to display His grace in the creating of children in His own image and glory. And at the
Cross the foundation was laid which was to make this possible and actual.

"It is finished." What was finished? The answer to this question is a very full one, though many
excellent expositors have sought to limit the scope of these words and to confine them strictly to
a single application. We are told it was the prophecies concerning the sufferings of Jesus which
were finished, and that He referred only to this. It is readily granted that the immediate reference
was to the Messianic predictions, yet we think there are good and sufficient reasons for not
confining our Lord's words here to them. Yea, to us it seems certain that Christ referred specially
to His sacrificial work, for all Scripture concerning His suffering and shame was not yet fulfilled.
There remained the dismissal of His spirit into the hands of the Father (Psa 31:5); there remained
the "piercing" with the spear (Zec 12:10: and note that the word used in Psalm 22:16 for the

piercing of His hands and feet—the act of crucifixion—is a different one); there still remained the preserving of His bones unbroken (Psa 34:20), and the burial in the rich man's grave (Isa 53:9).

"It is finished." What was finished? We answer His sacrificial work. It is true there yet remained the act of death itself, which was necessary for the making of atonement. But, as is so often the case here in John's Gospel wherein our text is found (cf. Joh 12:23, 31; 13:31; 16:5; 17:4), the Lord here speaks of the completion of His work. Moreover, it must be remembered that the three hours darkness was already past, the awful cup had already been drained, His precious blood had already been shed, the outpoured wrath of God had already been endured; and these are the primary elements in the making of propitiation. The sacrificial work of Jesus, then, was completed, excepting only the act of death which followed immediately. But, as we shall see, the completing of the sacrificial work made an end of several things.

"It is finished."
1. Here we see the accomplished fulfillment of all the prophecies which had been written of Him here He should die. This is the immediate thought of the context: "When Jesus therefore had received the vinegar, He said, It is finished" (John 19:30). Centuries beforehand, the prophets of God had described step by step the humiliation and suffering which the coming Savior should undergo. One by one these had been fulfilled, wonderfully fulfilled, fulfilled to the very letter. Had prophecy declared that He should be the "woman's seed" (Gen 3:15), then He was "born of a woman" (Gal 4:4). Had prophecy announced that His mother should be a "virgin" (Isa 7:14), then was it literally fulfilled (Mat 1:18). Had prophecy revealed that He should be of the seed of Abraham (Gen 22:18), then mark its fulfillment (Mat 1:1). Had prophecy made it known that He

Prophecy said that He should be named before He was born (Isa 49:1), then so it came to pass (Luke 1:30-31). Had prophecy foretold that He should be born in Bethlehem of Judea (Mic 5:2), then mark how this very village was His birthplace. Had prophecy forewarned that His birth should entail sorrowing for others (Jer 31:15), then behold its tragic fulfillment (Mat 2:14-18). Had prophecy foreshown that the Messiah should appear before the scepter of tribal ascendancy had departed from Judah (Gen 49:10), then so He did, for though the ten tribes were in captivity, Judah was still in the land at the time of His advent. Had prophecy referred to the flight into Egypt and the subsequent return into Palestine, (Hose 11:1 and cf. Isa 49:3, 6), then so it came to pass (Mat 2:1415).

Prophecy made mention of one going before Christ to make ready His way (Mal 3:1), then see its fulfillment in the person of John the Baptist. Had prophecy made it known that at the Messiah's appearing "the eyes of the blind shall be opened, and the ears of the deaf shall be unstopped, then shall the lame man leap as a hart, and the tongue of the dumb sing" (Isa 35:56), then read through the four Gospels and see how blessedly this proved true. Had prophecy spoken of Him as "poor and needy" (Psa 40:17, see beginning of Psalm), then behold Him not having where to lay His head. Had prophecy intimated that He should speak in "parables" (Psa 78:2), then such was frequently His method of teaching. Had prophecy depicted Him stilling the tempest (Psa 107:29), then this is exactly what He did. Had prophecy heralded His "triumphal entry" into Jerusalem (Zec 9:9), then so it came to pass!

Prophecy announced that His person should be despised (Isa 53:3), that He should be rejected by the Jews (Isa 8:14), that He should be "hated without a cause" (Psa 69:4), then sad to say, such was precisely the case. Had prophecy painted the whole picture of His degradation and crucifixion, then was it vividly reproduced. There had been the betrayal by a familiar friend, the forsaking by His disciples, the being led to the slaughter, the being taken to judgment, the appearing of false witnesses against Him, the refusal on His part to make defense, the establishing of His innocence, the unjust condemnation, the sentence of capital punishment passed upon Him, the literal piercing of His hands and feet, the being numbered with transgressors, the mockery of the crowd, the casting lots for His garments—all predicted centuries beforehand, and all fulfilled to the very letter. The last prophecy of all which remained here He committed His Spirit into the hands of His Father, had now been fulfilled. He cried "I thirst," and after the tendering of the vinegar and gall, all was now "accomplished"; and as the Lord Jesus reviewed the entire scope of the prophetic Word and saw its full realization, He cried,

"It is finished"!
It only remains for us to point out that as there was a complete set of prophecies which had to do with the first advent of Jesus, so also is there a complete set of prophecies which have to do with His second advent—the latter as definite, as personal, and as comprehensive in their scope as the former. As then we see the actual fulfillment of those which had to do with His first coming to the earth, we may look forward with absolute confidence and assurance to the fulfillment of those which have to do with His second coming. And, as we have seen that the former set of prophecies were fulfilled literally and personally, so also must we expect the latter set to be. To grant the literal fulfillment of the former, and then to seek to spiritualize and symbolize the latter, is not only grossly inconsistent and illogical, but is highly injurious to us and deeply dishonoring to God and to His Word.

"It is finished."
2. Here we see the completion of His sufferings. But what tongue or pen can describe the sufferings of Jesus? The anguish, physical, mental, and spiritual, which He endured! Appropriately was He designated "the man of sorrows": suffering at the hands of men, at the hands of Satan, and at the hands of God. Pain inflicted upon Him by enemies and friends alike. From the beginning He walked the shadows which the Cross cast His path. "I am afflicted and ready to die from my youth up" (Psa 88:15). What a light this throws on His earlier years! Who can say how much is contained in those words? For us, an impenetrable veil is cast over the future; none of us knows what a day may bring forth.

But Jesus knew the end from the beginning! One has only to read through the Gospels to learn how the awful Cross was ever before Him. At the marriage-feast of Cana, where all was gladness and merriment, He makes solemn reference to "his hour" not yet come. When Nicodemus interviewed Him at night, the Savior referred to the "lifting up of the Son of man." When James and John came to request from Him the two places of honor in His coming kingdom, He made mention of the "cup" which He had to drink, and of the "baptism" wherewith He must be baptized. When Peter confessed that He was the Christ, the Son of the living God, He turned to His disciples and began to show unto them "how that he must go unto Jerusalem, and suffer many things of the elders and chief priests and scribes, and be killed, and be raised again the third day" (Mat 16:21). When Moses and Elijah stood with Him on the Mount of

Transfiguration, it was to speak of "his decease which he should accomplish at Jerusalem" (Luke 9:31).

If it is true we are quite unable to estimate the sufferings of Christ due to the anticipation of the Cross, still less can we fathom the dread reality itself. The physical sufferings were excruciating, but even this was as nothing compared with His anguish of soul. To a consideration of these sufferings we have already devoted several paragraphs in previous chapters, yet we make no apology in turning to them again. We cannot contemplate too often what Jesus endured to secure our salvation. The better we are acquainted with His sufferings, and the more frequently we meditate thereon, the warmer will be our love and the deeper our gratitude.
At last the closing hours have come. There had been the terrible experience in Gethsemane followed by the appearing before Caiaphas, before Pilate, before Herod, and back again before Pilate. There had been the scourging and mocking by the brutal soldiers; the journey to Calvary; the fastening of His hands and feet to the cruel tree. There had been the reviling of the priests, the crowd, and the two thieves crucified with Him.

There had been the awful cloud that hid from the Father's face, which wrung from Him the bitter cry, "My God, my God, why hast thou forsaken me?" There had been the parched lips which drew from Him the exclamation "I thirst." There had been the fearful conflict with the power of darkness as the serpent "bruised" His heel. But now the suffering is ended. The Lord has bruised Him; man, and Devil have done their worst. The cup has been drained. The awful storm of God's wrath has spent itself. The darkness is ended. The sword of divine justice is done. The wages of sin have been paid. The prophecies of His sufferings are all fulfilled. The Cross has been "endured." Divine holiness has been fully satisfied (Isa 53:11). With a cry of triumph—a loud cry, a cry which reverberated throughout the entire universe—Jesus exclaims, "It is finished." The shame, the suffering and agony, are past. Never again shall He experience pain. Never again shall He endure the contradiction of sinners against Himself. Never again shall He be in the hands of Satan. Never again shall the light of God's countenance be hidden from Him. Blessed be God, all that is finished! "It is finished."

Jesus is concerned in the work of Redemption: He was the One who came here to die for sinners. He is the One who now gives spiritual illumination and understanding, and guides into the truth. Before the Lord Jesus came to this earth, a definite work was committed to Him. In the volume of the book it was written of Him, and He came to do the recorded will of God. Even as a boy of twelve the "Father's business" was before His heart and occupied His attention. Again, in John 5:36 we find Him saying, "But I have greater witness than that of John: for the works which the Father hath given me to finish, the same works that I do." And on the last night before His death, in that wonderful high priestly prayer, we find Him saying, "I have glorified thee on the earth: I have finished the work which thou gavest me to do" (John 17:4).

The mission upon which God had sent His Son into the world was now accomplished. It was not actually finished till He breathed His last, but death was only an instant ahead, and in anticipation of it He cries "It is finished." The demanding work is done. The divinely-given task is performed. A work more honorable and momentous than ever entrusted to man or angels, has been completed. That for which He had left heaven's glory that for which He had taken upon Him the form of a servant, that for which He had remained upon earth for thirty-three years to do, was now consummated. Nothing remained to be added. The goal of the Incarnation is reached. With what joyous triumph must He here have viewed the costly work which, committed to Him, had now been perfected!

"It is finished." The mission upon which God had sent His Son into the world was accomplished. That which had been eternally purposed had come to pass. The plan of God had been fully carried out.

Because He is the Most High, God's will, cannot be thwarted. Because He is supreme, God's counsel must stand. Because He is almighty, God's purpose cannot be overthrown.

"But he is in one mind, and who can turn him? And what his soul desireth, even that he doeth" (Job 23:13). "I know that thou canst do everything, and that no thought can be withholding from thee" (Job 42:2). "But our God is in the heavens: He hath done whatsoever he hath pleased" (Psa 115:3). "There is no wisdom nor understanding nor counsel against the Lord" (Pro 21:30). "For the Lord of hosts hath purposed, and who shall disannul it? And His hand is stretched out, and who shall turn it back?" (Isa 14:27). "Remember the former things of old: for I am God, and there is none else; I am God, and there is none like me: Declaring the end from the beginning, and from ancient times the things that are not yet done, saying, My counsel shall stand, and I will do all my pleasure" (Isa 46:9-10). "And all the inhabitants of the earth are reputed as nothing: and he doeth according to his will in the army of heaven, and among the inhabitants of the earth: and none can stay his hand, or say unto him, What doest thou?" (Dan 4:35). And, in the triumphant cry of the Jesus— "It is finished"—we have a prophecy and pledge of the ultimate carrying out of God's plan completely. At the end of time, when everything is wound up, and God's purpose has been fully consummated, when everything has been done which He before determined should be done, then shall it be said again, "It is finished."

"It is finished."

4. Here we see the accomplishment of the Atonement. Above we have spoken of Christ reaching the goal of the Incarnation, and of the consummation of His mission to the earth; what that goal and mission was, the Scriptures plainly reveal. The Son of Man came here "to seek and to save that which was lost" (Luke 19:10). Christ Jesus came into the world "to save sinners" (1Ti 1:15). God sent forth His Son, born of a woman, "to redeem them that were under the law" (Gal 4:5). He was manifested "to take away our sins" (1Jo 3:5). And all this involved the Cross. The "lost" which He came to seek could only be found there—in the place of death and under the condemnation of God. Sinners could be "saved" only by One taking their place and bearing their iniquities. They who were under the Law could be "redeemed" only by Another fulfilling its requirements and suffering its curse. Our sins could be "taken away" only by their being blotted out by the precious blood of Christ. The demands of justice must be met; the requirements of God's holiness must be satisfied; the awful debt we incurred must be paid. And on the Cross, this was done; done by none less than the Son of God; done perfectly; done once for all.

"It is finished."

That to which so many types looked forward, was now accomplished. A covering from sin and its shame, typified by the coats of skin with which the Lord God clothed our first parents, was now provided. The more excellent sacrifice, typified by Abel's lamb, had now been offered. A shelter from the storm of divine judgment, typified by the Ark of Noah, was now furnished. The only-begotten and well-beloved Son, typified by Abraham's offering up of Isaac, had already been placed upon the altar. A protection from the avenging angel, typified by the shed blood of the Passover-lamb, was now supplied. A cure from the serpent's bite, typified by the serpent of brass upon the pole, was now made ready for sinners. The providing of a life-giving fountain, typified by Moses striking the rock, was now affected.

"It is finished." The Greek word here, teleo, is translated variously in the New Testament. A glance at some of the different renderings in other passages will enable us to discern the fullness and finality of the term used by Jesus. In Matthew 11:1, teleo is rendered as follows, "When Jesus had made an end of commanding his twelve disciples, he departed thence." In Matthew 17:24 it is rendered, "They that received tribute money came to Peter, and said, Doth not your master pay tribute?" In Luke 2:39, it is rendered, "And when they had performed all things according to the Law of the Lord, they returned into Galilee." In Luke 18:31, it is rendered, "All things that are written by the prophets concerning the Son shall be accomplished."

"It is finished." He cried: it is "made an end of"; it is "paid"; it is "performed"; it is "accomplished." What was made an end of? —our sins and their guilt. What was "paid?"—the price of our redemption. What was "performed?"—the utmost requirements of the Law. What was "accomplished?"—the work which the Father had given Him to do. What was "finished?"— the making of atonement. God has furnished at least four proofs that Christ did finish the work which was given Him to do. First, in the rending of the veil, which showed that the way to God was now open. Second, in the raising of Christ from the dead, which evidenced that God had accepted His sacrifice. Third, the exaltation of Christ to His own right hand, which demonstrated the value of Christ's work and the Father's delight in His person. Fourth, the sending to earth of the Holy Spirit to apply the virtues and benefits of Christ's atoning death.

"It is finished." What was "finished?"—the work of atonement. What is the value of that to us? This: to the sinner, it is a message of glad tidings. All that a Holy God requires has been done. Nothing is left for the sinner to add. No works from us are demanded as the price of our salvation. All that is necessary for the sinner is to rest now by faith upon what Christ did. "The gift of God is eternal life through Jesus Christ our Lord" (Rom 6:23). To the believer, the knowledge that the atoning work of Christ is finished brings a sweet relief over against all the defects and imperfections of his services. There is nothing "finished" that we do: all our duties are imperfect. There is much of sin and vanity in the very best of our efforts, but the grand relief is that we are "complete" in Christ (Col 2:10)! Christ and His finished work are the ground of all our hopes. "It is finished."

5. Here we see the end of our sins. The sins of the believer, all of them, were transferred to the Jesus. As the Scripture says, "The Lord hath laid on him the iniquities of us all" (Isa 53:6). If then God laid my iniquities on Christ, they are no longer on me. Sin there is in me, for the old Adamic nature remains in the believer till death or till Christ's return, should He come before I die; but there is no sin on me. This distinction between sin in and sin on, is a vital one, and there should be little difficulty in apprehending it. If I were to say the judge passed sentence on a criminal, and that he is now under sentence of death, everyone would understand what I meant. In like manner, everyone out of Christ has the sentence of God's condemnation resting upon him. But when a sinner believes in the Lord Jesus, and receives Him as his Lord and Master, obey the salvation message according to (Acts 2:38-39) he is no longer "under condemnation"—

sin is no longer on him, that is, the guilt, the condemnation, the penalty of sin, is no longer upon him. And why? Because Christ bore our sins in His own body on the tree (1Pe 2:24)—the guilt, condemnation, and penalty of our sins, was transferred to our substitute. Hence, because my sins were transferred to Christ, they are no more upon me.

This precious truth was strikingly illustrated in Old Testament times regarding Israel's annual Day of Atonement. On that day, Aaron, the high priest (a type of Christ), made satisfaction to God for the sins which Israel had committed during the previous year. The way this was done is described in Leviticus 16. Two goats were taken and presented before the Lord at the door of the tabernacle: this was before anything was done with them: it represented Christ being sent and presenting Himself, offering to come into this world and be the Savior of sinners. One of the goats was then taken and killed, and its blood was carried into the tabernacle, within the veil, into the Holy of Holies, and there it was sprinkled before and upon the mercy seat—foreshadowing Christ offering Himself as a sacrifice, to meet the demands of His justice and satisfy the requirements of His holiness.

Then we read that Aaron came out of the tabernacle and laid both his hands upon the head of the second (living) goat— signifying an act of identification by which Aaron is the representative of the whole nation, identified the people with it, acknowledging that its doom was what their sins merited, and which, today, corresponds with the hands of faith laying hold of Christ and identifying ourselves with Him in His Death. Having laid his hands on the head of the live goat, Aaron now confessed over him "all the iniquities of the children of Israel, and all their transgressions in all their sins, putting them upon the head of the goat" (Lev 16:21). Thus, were Israel's sins transferred to their substitute. Finally, we are told, "And the goat shall bear upon him all their iniquities unto a land not inhabited: and he shall let go the goat in the wilderness" (Lev 16:22). The goat bearing Israel's sins, was taken unto an uninhabited wilderness, and the people of God saw him and their sins no more! In type this was Christ taking our sins into that desolate land where God was not and there making an end of them. The Cross of Christ then is the grave of our sins!

"It is finished."
6. Here we see the fulfillment of the Law's requirements. "The law is holy, and the commandment holy, and just and good" (Rom 7:12). How could it be anything less when Jehovah Himself had framed and given it! The fault lay not in the Law but in man who, being depraved and sinful, could not keep it. Yet that Law must be kept, and kept by a man, so that the Law might be honored and magnified, and its giver vindicated. Therefore, we read, "For what the law could not do, in that it was weak through the flesh, God sending his own Son, in the likeness of sinful flesh, and for sin, condemned sin in the flesh: that the righteousness of the law might be fulfilled in [not by] us, who walk not after flesh, but after the Spirit" (Rom 8:3-4). The "weakness" here is that of fallen man. The sending forth of God's Son in the likeness of sin's flesh (Greek) refers to the Incarnation: as we read in another Scripture, "God sent forth his Son, born of a woman, born under the law, that he might redeem them that were under the law" (Gal 4:4-5 RV). Yes, the Jesus was born "under the law," born under it that He might keep it perfectly in thought, word, and deed. "Think not that I am come to destroy the law, or the prophets: I am not come to destroy, but to fulfill" (Mat 5:17); such was His claim.

But not only did Jesus keep the precepts of the Law, He also suffered its penalty and endured its curse. We had broken it, and taking our place, He must receive its just sentence. Having received its penalty and endured its curse, the demands of the Law are fully met, and justice is satisfied. Therefore, is it written of believers, "Christ hath redeemed us from the curse of the law, being made a curse for us" (Gal 3:13). And again, "For Christ is the end of the law for righteousness to everyone that believeth" (Rom 10:4). And yet again, "For ye are not under the law, but under grace" (Rom 6:14). "It is finished." "Free from the Law, Jesus hath bled, and there is remission, cursed by the law and bruised by the fall, Grace hath redeemed us once for all."

7. Here we see the destruction of Satan's power. See it by faith. The Cross sounded the death of the devil's power. To human appearances it looked like the moment of his greatest triumph, yet, it was the hour of his ultimate defeat. In view of the Cross Jesus declared, "Now is the judgment of this world: now shall the prince of this world be cast out" (Joh 12:31). It is true that Satan has not yet been chained and cast into the bottomless pit, nevertheless, sentence has been passed (though not yet executed); his doom is certain; and his power is already broken so far as believers are concerned.

For the Christian, the devil is a vanquished foe. He was defeated by Christ at the Cross— "that through death he might destroy him that had the power of death, that is, the devil" (Hebrew 2:14). Believers have already been "delivered from the power of darkness" and translated into the kingdom of God's dear Son (Col 1:13). Satan, then, should be treated as a defeated enemy. No longer has he any legitimate claim upon us. Once we were his lawful "captives"; but now God worketh in us both to will and to do of His good pleasure. All that we now must do is to "resist the devil," and the promise is, "he will flee from you" (James 4:7).

"It is finished." Here was the triumphant answer to the rage of man and the enmity of Satan. It tells of the perfect work which meets sin in the place of judgment. All was completed just as God would have it, just as the prophets had foretold, just as the Old Testament ceremonial had foreshadowed, just as divine holiness demanded, and just as sinners needed. How strikingly appropriate is this sixth Cross-utterance of Jesus found in John's Gospel—the Gospel which displays the glory of Christ's deity! He seals it with His own words, attesting it is complete, and giving it the all-sufficient sanction of His own approval. Jesus says, "It is finished"—who then dare doubt or question it.

"It is finished." Reader, do you believe it? or, are you trying to add something of your own to the finished work of Christ to secure the favor of God? All you must do is to accept the pardon which He purchased. God is satisfied with His work on the cross, why are not you? Sinner, the moment you believe Jesus' testimony that it is finished, that moment every sin you have committed is blotted out, and you stand accepted in Christ! O would you not like to possess the assurance that there is nothing between your soul and God? Would you not like to know that every sin had been atoned for and put away? Then believe what God's Word says about Christ's death. Rest not on your feelings and experiences but on the written Word. There is only one way of finding peace, deliverance, wholeness, salvation, victory over the "it" and that is through faith in the shed blood of Jesus the of Lamb God. It is time to "Get Rid of "it", Before "it" Gets Rid of You".

"It is finished." Do you really believe it? Or, are you endeavoring to add something of your own to it and thus merit the favor of God? By continuing to hold on and struggle, seeking other sources to deal with the "it" in your life, you are nullifying the finished work of Christ by your own miserable additions to it!". The Gospel of God's grace, and the finished work of Christ is sufficient for our souls to rest upon. In the pages of this book, God uses forceful object lessons and His Word to show you, "How to Get Rid of "it", before "it" Gets Rid of You". It is a grave mistake not to embrace the Word of God, and cast yourself by faith upon what Christ had done for you.

Victory was given to us by way of the cross. Whatever your "it" or "its" might be, "it" has come to kill, steal and destroy you. Make a conscious effort to explore this information given in this book and expose the enemy of your soul. Let's "Get Rid of "it". After all, "It is Finished"

CHAPTER ONE

What is "it"?

We are all created with a basic need to be loved. God created us to both give and receive love, but though damaged emotions, our capacity to receive love can be dramatically hindered. Ignorance of God's love will also hinder us from receiving the great and glorious love that He has for us. **The root of most "its" is a lack of love being received by that person.** Many of us have been damaged emotionally by rejection, abandonment, abuse, etc., and thereby our capacity to receive love has been reduced. **Only an emotionally healthy person is capable of both giving and receiving love as God intended.**

Self-worth issues can hinder love

Self-worth issues are rooted in believing that we are not worthy or deserve to be loved. When we believe that we are unlovable, we will unconsciously reject any love that comes our way. We won't believe the love, because we believe in our hearts that we are not worthy. **Self-worth issues are all rooted in our failing to see who we really are in Christ.**

If you walked into a gallery of world-class art, and pointed to a painting, saying, "That is the ugliest thing I've ever seen! Who painted that??" Now let's say the artist was standing right next to you. How do you think that would make him feel? Do you realize we are the artwork of God, a special painting crafted together by the master painter? Do you think it brings Him honor when we look down on ourselves? **We need to stop putting down what God has made.**

Many times, we have self-unforgiveness issues because we blame ourselves for something, or we've done something we deeply regret, and we simply cannot let it go. We need to realize that Jesus has forgiven us of all our failures, and we need to start seeing ourselves as forgiven. Otherwise, we're denying the work of Christ in our life! **If God forgave you, and you're still beating yourself up, then you don't really believe what Jesus did for you.** It's that simple!

Just as we must forgive others (see Matthew 18:21-35), we need to forgive ourselves just the same. Self-hate has been known to be the root behind diseases such as lupus and Crohn's disease, as well as other auto-immune diseases. We need to stop holding ourselves accountable for that which Jesus has set us free from.

If we want to be in faith, we need to BELIEVE what Jesus did for us, and part of that believing is seeing ourselves as forgiven and clothed with the righteousness of God, which is upon all who believe in the finished work of Christ. Without faith, it is impossible to please God (see Hebrews 11:6), so if you want to please God, start taking the finished work of the cross seriously, and begin to see yourself as forgiven, washed clean, and clothed in the righteousness of God. For the righteousness (right standing with God) is upon all who believe:

> *"Even the righteousness of God which is by faith of Jesus Christ unto all and upon all them that believe..." (Romans 3:22 KJV)*

Unforgiveness is rooted in a lack of realization of how much God has forgiven us, and therefore we're not thankful for the steep and terrible price that Jesus paid for our own failures. Therefore, it is so important to mediate on what Jesus did for us, until it transforms our heart. The message of Jesus' work for us is what causes faith to arise in our hearts and transforms us from the inside out (read Romans 10:8-17).

Learning to see yourself as God sees you, and forgive yourself because you want to please God and be in faith and be thankful for what Jesus did for you, is the biggest step in overcoming self-worth issues. Of course, there are spirits that may need to be driven out as well, such as self-hate, guilt, condemnation, etc.

Receiving the love God has for us

When it comes to God's love for us, that's obvious, considering how He loves even the sinner so much that Jesus came to die for them. Anybody who knows the message of the cross, has some knowledge of God's love for us. However, many times, we blame God for our problems, and so we don't believe the love that He has for us. Not only do we blame Him for our problems, many times we think that God gave us the sickness or problem in our life to teach us something. Nothing could be further from the truth! Jesus tells us clearly who came to kill, steal, and destroy, and who came so that we could have life and have it in abundance.

> *"The thief cometh not, but for to steal, and to kill, and to destroy: I am come that they might have life, and that they might have it more abundantly." (John 10:10 KJV)*

If we are going to receive the love that God has for us, we need to get our thinking straightened out. He's not the one behind our problems, but rather Jesus paid the full price so that we can be forgiven all our sins, both physically and emotionally healed, and blessed.

> *"When the even was come, they brought unto him many that were possessed with devils: and he cast out the spirits with his word, and healed all that were*

Look at how good God's heart is toward mankind! Not only did Jesus heal them, but He proved the blessings of the covenant we have with Him today concerning our healing and deliverance. Isn't He good toward us? **The reason why things happen to us, is because we live in a fallen world that is under the control of the evil one.** It's not God's fault. He loves you. Jesus died for you.

Settling the fact that God loves you and is good toward you is crucial to restoring your God-given capacity to receive His love. If you can't receive His love, then you need to stop and ask yourself four questions:

1. Am I blaming God for anything bad that happened to me?

2. Have I been emotionally wounded in such a way that it is hindering my ability to freely receive love as God intended me to?

3. Do I have knowledge and revelation of how much God loves me? Do I have a solid Biblical understanding of how I am loved with the same kind of love that the Father has for Jesus?

4. Is there a self-worth issue that makes me feel unworthy to be loved?

Settling these issues lays a foundation for breaking free from the power of the "IT". You must repair the damage and faulty thinking which hinders your ability to receive the love that God has for you.

How do you know if you are receiving God's love or if it's hindered? **If you are not passionate about Jesus, then somewhere your ability to receive His love is hindered.**

If you are living a life without receiving God's love in your heart daily, you are missing out on the most fulfilling life you can have here on this earth. To know God's love, which surpasses all understanding (see Philippians 4:7), dispels all our fears and gives us a sense of peace and joy that we could never otherwise know.

What exactly is "it"?

An "it" is formed when we try to use something other than God, to meet our need to be loved. When our ability to receive God's love into our hearts is hindered, we will feel like something is missing, and seek to fill that void with something else. When that thing, whatever it might be, fills that void, we grow to love "it" because it's meeting a need. Over time, we establish a relationship with that thing, and when it comes time to depart, it's like breaking up a relationship. That's why the "it" is so destructive; we've relied on that thing to meet a need and we've established a relationship with it. Now when it's time to break up the love, it isn't so easy to say goodbye.

One widespread problem that we see when we try to deal with "it", is where we give up one "it" successfully, only to find yourself with another "it". We might quit drinking only to start overeating, for example. We might think we're finding victory, but all we're really doing is trading one "it" for another "it". This is because something must fill the love-void in our hearts, and if it's not one thing, it will be another.

What about cutting or self-harm?

Cutting or self-mutation is a special type of "it", where there's a need to either release pain in a person's heart or the person believes that they deserve to be punished for their failures. In these cases, the person certainly has an issue receiving the love that God has for them but there's another type of root that needs to be addressed as well. There's emotional pain or guilt that the person is dealing with that needs to be resolved. Finding out what happened and receiving Christ's truth concerning those areas is important for their healing. Any bondage involving guilt will need to be resolved through realizing and accepting the work of Christ on the cross for that person and they will likely need spirits of guilt, condemnation, self-hate, etc. driven out in Jesus' name. Again, getting the person to see them self for who they really are in Christ, forgiven, loved, and blessed, is crucial to lasting freedom from self-hate issues.

See yourself as lovable!

The key in uprooting most "its" is to deal with the underlying issues which are limiting their capacity to freely receive love from God and others, along with dealing with any self-worth issues by establishing an understanding of your true identity in Christ. **Coming to a place where you believe you are lovable is key to receiving love in general**, so dealing with self-worth issues is an important key to breaking down the walls which keep us from feeling loved. The only way to obtain a true sense of worth and value is to get a revelation of how much you are loved by God, who sent His son Jesus to die for you.

Discovering the root

To discover the root of your "it", you need to get real honest with yourself. Many times, we are in denial about the pain we are feeling. Figuring out what is the root of a bondage is all about asking the right questions, and that is especially important when it comes to uprooting an "it". Why don't we feel loved? Do we feel unlovable? (Let's stop right there; if we feel unlovable, then you've just discovered a self-worth issue that will need to be addressed.) Are you passionate about Jesus? If not, then something in hindering you from realizing how much you are loved by Him who died for you. Do you see yourself as forgiven and loved by the God because of what He did for you?

As you discover emotional wounds, you'll need to forgive (others, yourself, and God) and invite Jesus to come and heal the damage in your heart. If you don't realize how much God loves you, then you'll need to spend some time learning about what Jesus did for you on the cross, and what a terrible price He paid because He loved you so very much. Often breaking out of an "it" is a combination of emotional healing, learning about who you are in Christ, forgiving (yourself, others, and God), overcoming self-worth issues by changing how you see yourself (in light of how God sees and loves you), and casting out any spirits that came in and are enforcing the destructive behavior. Spirits behind guilt, condemnation, etc. also need to be driven out, as they seek to keep us from fully seeing what Jesus did for us on the cross.

Dealing with the issues underlying an "it" is key to uprooting it permanently. If you want lasting freedom and wholeness in this area of your life, you will have to deal with the issues that have limited your capacity to receive love, especially the love that God has for you.

CHAPTER TWO

The "it" of Attitudes

DEFINTION: An attitude is how you think about and respond to something or someone.

FACTS ABOUT ATTITUDES:

Bad attitudes can be learned behaviors. For example, your parent may have been prejudice against a certain race of people and taught you to have the same attitude. If you were raised in a critical environment, you may develop a critical spirit.

Bad attitudes can result from negative experiences. For example, if you are a black man who was assaulted by a Mexican, you may develop a negative attitude towards all Mexicans because of your experience.

God is concerned about attitudes. Christ's teachings in Matthew 5, known as the Sermon on the Mount, confirms this when He declares that we are to be meek, merciful, peacemakers, etc. The Fruit of the Holy Spirit that is to be manifested in your life are attitudes of love, joy, peace, patience, kindness, goodness, faithfulness, gentleness, and self-control.

Your attitude should always be Christ-like. In any circumstance and towards any person, a believer should always manifest positive Christ-like attitudes.

DEALING WITH ATTITUDES:

Take responsibility for your attitudes. You will never be able to conquer sinful attitudes until you stop blaming them on others.

Ask forgiveness for bad attitudes. Ask God to forgive you and ask forgiveness from those who were impacted by your negative attitudes.

Ask God to develop the Fruit of the Spirit in your life. These include "... *love, joy, peace, patience, kindness, goodness, faithfulness, gentleness, and self-control" (Galatians 5:22-23).* Put off your bad attitudes and put these on!

WHAT GOD'S WORD SAYS ABOUT ATTITUDES:

Attitudes in general.

Get rid of all bitterness, rage and anger, brawling and slander, along with every form of malice. Be kind and compassionate to one another, forgiving each other, just as in Christ God forgave you. (Ephesians 4:31-32)

Attitudes in the home.

Wives, submit to your husband as to the Lord. For the husband is the head of the wife as Christ is the head of the church, his body, of which he is the Savior. Now as the church submits to Christ, so also wives should submit to their husbands in everything. Husbands, love your wives, just as Christ loved the church and gave himself up for her to make her holy, cleansing her by the washing with water through the word, and to present her to himself as a radiant church, without stain or wrinkle or any other blemish, but holy and blameless. In this same way, husbands ought to love their wives as their own bodies. He who loves his wife loves himself. (Ephesians 5:22-29)

Children, obey your parents in the Lord, for this is right. "Honor your father and mother"-which is the first commandment with a promise--"that it may go well with you and that you may enjoy long life on the earth." Fathers, do not exasperate your children; instead, bring them up in the training and instruction of the Lord. (Ephesians 6:1-4)

Attitudes towards Christian brothers and sisters.

Be devoted to one another in brotherly love. Honor one another above yourselves. (Romans 12:10)

Do nothing out of selfish ambition or vain conceit, but in humility consider others better than yourselves. Each of you should look not only to your own interests, but also to the interests of others. Your attitude should be the same as that of Christ Jesus... (Philippians 2:3-5)

Do not rebuke an older man harshly, but exhort him as if he were your father. Treat younger men as brothers, older women as mothers, and younger women as sisters, with absolute purity. (1 Timothy 5:1-2)

Attitudes on the job.

Slaves, obey your earthly masters with respect and fear, and with sincerity of heart, just as you would obey Christ. Obey them not only to win their favor when their eye is on you, but like slaves of Christ, doing the will of God from your heart. Serve wholeheartedly, as if you were serving the Lord, not men, because you know that the Lord will reward everyone for whatever good he does, whether he is slave or free. And masters, treat your slaves in the same way. Do not threaten them, since you know that he who is both their Master and yours is in heaven, and there is no favoritism with him. (Ephesians 6:5-9)

Attitudes towards authority.

Everyone must submit himself to the governing authorities, for there is no authority except that which God has established. The authorities that exist have been established by God. Consequently, he who rebels against the authority is rebelling against what God has instituted, and those who do so will bring judgment on themselves. (Romans 13:1-3)

I urge, then, first of all, that requests, prayers, intercession and thanksgiving be made for everyone--for kings and all those in authority, that we may live peaceful and quiet lives in all godliness and holiness. (1 Timothy 2:1-2)

Obey your leaders and submit to their authority. They keep watch over you as men who must give an account. Obey them so that their work will be a joy, not a burden, for that would be of no advantage to you. (Hebrews 13:17)

Attitudes towards those who have wronged you.

For if you forgive men when they sin against you, your heavenly Father will also forgive you. But if you do not forgive men their sins, your Father will not forgive your sins. (Matthew 6:14-15)

Attitudes towards those of other races or socio-economic levels.

For who makes you different from anyone else? What do you have that you did not receive? And if you did receive it, why do you boast as though you did not? (1 Corinthians 4:7)

If you really keep the royal law found in Scripture, "Love your neighbor as yourself," you are doing right. But if you show favoritism, you sin and are convicted by the law as lawbreakers. (James 2:8-9)

Attitudes towards the unsaved.

...snatch others from the fire and save them; to others show mercy, mixed with fear-hating even the clothing stained by corrupted flesh. (Jude 23)

CHAPTER THREE

The "it" of Criticism and a Critical Spirit

DEFINITION: Being critical is to make and express assumptions about the moral and personal conduct of others. Having a critical spirit is to be guilty of this continuously, always criticizing and putting others down.

FACTS ABOUT CRITICISM AND A CRITICAL SPIRIT:

God is the judge. You are not to criticize others because God is the judge (Romans 14:12-13). When you take it upon yourself to judge others, you are trying to assume a function of God.

You will be judged the same way you judge others. Think about that when tempted to judge and criticize other people (Matthew 7:2).

When you criticize others, you condemn yourself. Very often, you are doing the same things you are criticizing others for--if not worse (Romans 2:1).

When you criticize your leaders, you are criticizing God. Israel criticized Moses and Aaron, but God viewed it as criticism of Himself because He had set these leaders in authority (Numbers 14:27).

DEALING WITH CRITICISM AND A CRITICAL SPIRIT:

Ask God to forgive your judgmental, critical spirit. Since Jesus said not to judge others, then it is a sin when you do.

Focus on dealing with issues in your own life. Instead of judging and criticizing others, focus on your own moral and spiritual condition (Matthew 7:1-5).

Ask God to help you guard what you say. David said, *"Set a guard over my mouth, O Lord, keep watch over the door of my lips" (Psalm 141:3).*

View others as God sees them. God sees you and others, not as you are, but as you have the capacity to become. Look at a person's potential, not their problems.

Do not accept criticism raised against you unless you believe it is justified. Simply tell the person, "Thank you for bringing that to my attention." If it is something legitimate, correct it. If not, forget it. When you are praised for something, do you not lift that praise to God since every good thing done in you and through you is because of Him? Lift unjustified criticism to Him in the same way.

WHAT GOD'S WORD SAYS ABOUT CRITICISM AND A CRITICAL SPIRIT:

For in the same way you judge others, you will be judged, and with the measure you use, it will be measured to you. Why do you look at the speck of sawdust in your brother's eye and pay no attention to the plank in your own eye? How can you say to your brother, 'Let me take the speck out of your eye," when all the time there is a plank in your own eye? You hypocrite, first take the plank out of your own eye, and then you will see clearly to remove the speck from your brother's eye. (Matthew 7:1-5)

Do not judge, and you will not be judged. Do not condemn, and you will not be condemned. (Luke 6:37)

And will not God bring about justice for his chosen ones, who cry out to him day and night? Will he keep putting them off? I tell you, he will see that they get justice, and quickly. (Luke 18:7-8)

You judge by human standards; I pass judgment on no one. But if I do judge, my decisions are right, because I am not alone. I stand with the Father, who sent me. (John 8:15-16)

For at whatever point you judge the other, you are condemning yourself, because you who pass judgment do the same things. (Romans 2:1)

So when you, a mere man, pass judgment on them and yet do the same things, do you think you will escape God's judgment? (Romans 2:3)

Accept him whose faith is weak, without passing judgment on disputable matters. (Romans 14:1)

You, then, why do you judge your brother? Or why do you look down on your brother? For we will all stand before God's judgment seat. (Romans 14:10)

Each of us will give an account of himself to God. Therefore let us stop passing judgment on one another. (Romans 14:12-13)

The spiritual man makes judgments about all things, but he himself is not subject to any man's judgment. (1 Corinthians 2:15)

I do not even judge myself. My conscience is clear, but that does not make me innocent. It is the Lord who judges me. Therefore judge nothing before the appointed time; wait till the Lord comes. (1 Corinthians 4:3-5)

Anyone who speaks against his brother or judges him speaks against the law and judges it. When you judge the law, you are not keeping it, but sitting judgment on it. There is only one Lawgiver and Judge, the one who is able to save and destroy. But you -- who are you to judge your neighbor? (James 4:11-12)

CHAPTER FOUR

The "it" of Impatience

DEFINITION: Impatience is defined as annoyance with aggravating circumstances or people. Patience, the opposite of impatience, is the ability to cheerfully bear an unbearable situation or person.

FACTS ABOUT IMPATIENCE:

Patience, the opposite of impatience, is referred to as longsuffering, perseverance, and endurance in various translations of the Bible.

God mandates that you have patience. You are to be longsuffering (patient) with joyfulness (Colossians 1:11). You are called to be longsuffering (Ephesians 4:2). You are to preach the Word of God with longsuffering (2 Timothy 4:2) and put on longsuffering as a spiritual quality (Colossians 3:12). Many verses in Proverbs extol the benefits of patience (Proverbs 14:29; 15:18; 16:32; 19:2,11; 15:18).

The Bible provides positive examples of patience. God is depicted as being patient and longsuffering in the following verses: Exodus 34:6; Numbers 14:18; Psalms 86:15; Romans 2:4. Patience was a quality evident in the ministry of the Apostle Paul (2 Timothy 3:10). James refers to the patience of the prophets and the long-suffering Job (James 5:10-11).

Impatience leads to wrong responses. Angry, hurtful words and actions often result from impatience.

When you are impatient with God, you are not trusting His timing and will for your life. Abraham became impatient and birthed Ishmael of his own flesh and created problems that last to this day. King Saul became impatient because Samuel didn't arrive on time, acted in haste, and it cost him the kingdom. What will impatience cost you?

Patience is a hallmark of true love. First Corinthians 13:4 states that true love is patient.

Patience is developed through tribulations. As you learn to develop patience in difficulties, it sets in motion an important spiritual process so that you can ... *"glory in tribulations also: knowing that tribulation worketh patience; And patience, experience; and experience, hope: And hope maketh not ashamed; because the love of God is shed abroad in our hearts by the Holy Ghost which is given unto us"* (Romans 5:3-5, KJV).

You are to make an effort to develop patience. 2 Peter 1:5-8 mandates: *"For this very reason, make every effort to add to your faith goodness; and to goodness, knowledge; and to knowledge, self-control; and to self-control, perseverance; and to perseverance, godliness; and to godliness, brotherly kindness; and to brotherly kindness, love. For if you possess these qualities in increasing measure, they will keep you from being ineffective and unproductive in your knowledge of our Lord Jesus Christ."*

DEALING WITH IMPATIENCE:

Ask God to forgive your impatience. Since God's Word mandates patience and long-suffering, then impatience is a sinful response to annoying people and circumstances. When you are impatient with God, you are not trusting His timing and will for your life.

Ask God to manifest the Fruit of the Holy Spirit in your life. One of the Fruit is long-suffering (patience*): "But the fruit of the Spirit is love, joy, peace, patience, kindness, goodness, faithfulness, gentleness and self-control" (Galatians 5:22-23).*

Develop self-control through spiritual growth. *"For this very reason, make every effort to add to your faith goodness; and to goodness, knowledge; and to knowledge, self-control; and to self-control, perseverance; and to perseverance, godliness; and to godliness, brotherly kindness; and to brotherly kindness, love. For if you possess these qualities in increasing measure, they will keep you from being ineffective and unproductive in your knowledge of our Lord Jesus Christ" (2 Peter 1:5-8).*

Identify and correct annoying circumstances. Some circumstances that trigger impatience can be corrected. Analyze the circumstances to see if there is a way to correct annoying situations so that you won't be tempted to be impatient. For example, if constant interruptions by the phone annoy you when you are working, let your calls go to voice mail. Set a certain time to return all calls after you are done working. Practical solutions to irritations like this can eliminate many annoying circumstances in life.

Forgive annoying people that contribute to your impatience responses. *"Therefore, as God's chosen people, holy and dearly loved, clothe yourselves with compassion, kindness, humility, gentleness and patience. Bear with each other and forgive whatever grievances you may have against one another. Forgive as the Lord forgave you" (Colossians 3:12-13).*

Take time to think before you speak or act. Is what you are about to say or do representative of a true believer or is it a response arising out of impatience?

WHAT GOD'S WORD SAYS ABOUT IMPATIENCE:

Be still before the Lord and wait patiently for him; do not fret when men succeed in their ways, when they carry out their wicked schemes. (Psalm 37:7)

I waited patiently for the Lord; he turned to me and heard my cry. He lifted me out of the slimy pit, out of the mud and mire; he set my feet on a rock and gave me a firm place to stand. (Psalm 40:1-2)

A patient man has great understanding, but a quick-tempered man displays folly. (Proverbs 14:29)

A hot-tempered man stirs up dissension, but a patient man calms a quarrel. (Proverbs 15:18)

Better a patient man than a warrior, a man who controls his temper than one who takes a city. (Proverbs 16:32)

It is not good to have zeal without knowledge, nor to be hasty and miss the way. (Proverbs 19:2)

A man's wisdom gives him patience; it is to his glory to overlook an offense. (Proverbs 19:11)

The end of a matter is better than its beginning, and patience is better than pride. Do not be quickly provoked in your spirit, for anger resides in the lap of fools. (Ecclesiastes 7:8-9)

And not only so, but we glory in tribulations also: knowing that tribulation worketh patience; And patience, experience; and experience, hope: And hope maketh not ashamed; because the love of God is shed abroad in our hearts by the Holy Ghost which is given unto us. (Romans 5:3-5, KJV)

Be joyful in hope, patient in affliction, faithful in prayer. (Romans 12:12)

Love is patient, love is kind. It does not envy, it does not boast, it is not proud. (1 Corinthians 13:4)

Rather, as servants of God we commend ourselves in every way: in great endurance; in troubles, hardships and distresses; in beatings, imprisonments and riots; in hard work, sleepless nights and hunger; in purity, understanding, patience and kindness; in the Holy Spirit and in sincere love; (2 Corinthians 6:3-7)

But the fruit of the Spirit is love, joy, peace, patience, kindness, goodness, faithfulness, gentleness and self-control. (Galatians 5:22-23)

As a prisoner for the Lord, then, I urge you to live a life worthy of the calling you have received. Be completely humble and gentle; be patient, bearing with one another in love. (Ephesians 4:1-2)

And we pray this in order that you may live a life worthy of the Lord and may please him in every way: bearing fruit in every good work, growing in the knowledge of God, being strengthened with all power according to his glorious might so that you may have great endurance and patience, and joyfully. (Colossians 1:10-11)

Therefore, as God's chosen people, holy and dearly loved, clothe yourselves with compassion, kindness, humility, gentleness and patience. Bear with each other and forgive whatever grievances you may have against one another. Forgive as the Lord forgave you. (Colossians 3:12-13)

And we urge you, brothers, warm those who are idle, encourage the timid, help the weak, be patient with everyone. (1 Thessalonians 5:14)

But you, O man of God, flee these things and pursue righteousness, godliness, faith, love, patience, gentleness. (1 Timothy 6:11, NKJV)

Preach the Word; be prepared in season and out of season; correct, rebuke and encourage--with great patience and careful instruction. (2 Timothy 4:2)

Therefore, we also, since we are surrounded by so great a cloud of witnesses, let us lay aside every weight, and the sin which so easily ensnares us, and let us run with endurance the race that is set before us. (Hebrews 12:1, NKJV)

Be patient, then, brothers, until the Lord's coming. See how the farmer waits for the land to yield its valuable crop and how patient he is for the autumn and spring rains. You too, be patient and stand firm, because the Lord's coming is near. (James 5:7-8)

Brothers, as an example of patience in the face of suffering, take the prophets who spoke in the name of the Lord. As you know, we consider blessed those who have persevered. You have heard of Job's perseverance and have seen what the Lord finally brought about. The Lord is full of compassion and mercy. (James 5:10-11)

But how is it to your credit if you receive a beating for doing wrong and endure it? But if you suffer for doing good and you endure it, this is commendable before God. To this you were called, because Christ suffered for you, leaving you an example, that you should follow in his steps. (1 Peter 2:20-21)

For this very reason, make every effort to add to your faith goodness; and to goodness, knowledge; and to knowledge, self-control; and to self-control, perseverance; and to perseverance, godliness; and to godliness, brotherly kindness; and to brotherly kindness, love. For if you possess these qualities in increasing measure, they will keep you from being ineffective and unproductive in your knowledge of our Lord Jesus Christ. (2 Peter 1:5-8)

CHAPTER FIVE

The "it" of Evil

DEFINITION: The dictionary defines evil as being morally bad. For believers, it is any act or thought that violates the Word of God. Other words for evil used in the Bible include iniquity, transgression, and sin.

FACTS ABOUT EVIL:

Evil exists everywhere. Since the fall of Satan from heaven and Adam and Eve's original sin, evil has been manifested in the world.

Evil is sin. The Bible calls evil "transgression, sin, and iniquity". Evil is the opposite of all that is good and is any act or thought that is contrary to God's Word.

You will encounter evil people and circumstances. Because you live in an evil world, you will confront evil people and evil circumstances. You cannot control the circumstances or the people, but you can control your attitudes and responses towards them and your involvement in evil.

DEALING WITH EVIL:

Realize that everyone is tempted. You are not the only one tempted to do wrong, but you must recognize where the temptation comes from and what to do about it (James 1:13-15). Reject it the minute it enters your mind.

Repent of evil. Acknowledge evil thoughts and actions as sin and repent of them. God is faithful to forgive you of confessed sins, but He goes beyond that to cleanse you from all unrighteousness when you come to Him seeking forgiveness (1 John 1:8-9).

Eliminate sinful practices. Reject every kind of evil--even the appearance of evil (1 Thessalonians 5:22 and Ephesians 5:3-17). Dispose of evil literature, photographs, pornography, music, and anything that has to do with the occult. Do not hang out where evil people congregate.

Be filled with the Holy Spirit. Learn to walk according to the guidance and dictates of the Holy Spirit who is resident within you. When you feel like something is wrong, that is the Holy Spirit warning you to avoid it (Ephesians 5:18).

Concentrate on pure things. Do not think about or give your attention to evil things. The Apostle Paul said: *"Finally, brothers, whatever is true, whatever is noble, whatever is right, whatever is pure, whatever is lovely, whatever is admirable--if anything is excellent or praiseworthy--think about such things" (Philippians 4:8).*

WHAT GOD'S WORD SAYS ABOUT EVIL:

The fear of the Lord--that is wisdom, and to shun evil is understanding. (Job 28:28)

Turn from evil and do good; then you will dwell in the land forever. (Psalm 37:27)

Deliver me, 0 my God, from the hand of the wicked, from the grasp of evil and cruel men. (Psalm 71:4)

Let not my heart be drawn to what is evil, to take part in wicked deeds with men who are evildoers; let me not eat of their delicacies. (Psalm 141:4)

Keep me from the snares they have laid for me, from the traps set by evildoers. (Psalm 141:9)

Do not be wise in your own eyes; fear the Lord and shun evil. (Proverbs 3:7)

Through the fear of the Lord a man avoids evil. (Proverbs 16:6)

In the paths of the wicked lie thorns and snares, but he who guards his soul stays far from them. (Proverbs 22:5)

Woe to those who call evil good and good evil, who put darkness for light and light for darkness, who put bitter for sweet and sweet for bitter. (Isaiah 5:20)

This is what the Lord says: "Maintain justice and do what is right, for my salvation is close at Your eye is the lamp of your body. When your eyes are good, your whole body also is full of light. But when they are bad, your body also is full of darkness. See to it then, that the light within you is not darkness." (Luke 11:34-35)

Everyone who does evil hates the light, and will not come into the light for fear that his deeds will be exposed. (John 3:20)

Hate what is evil; cling to what is good. (Romans 12:9)

Do not be overcome by evil, but overcome evil with good. (Romans 12:21)

Do not be misled: Bad company corrupts good character. (1 Corinthians 15:33)

But among you there must not be even a hint of sexual immorality, or of any kind of impurity, or of greed, because these are improper for God's holy people. Nor should there be obscenity, foolish talk or coarse joking, which are out of place, but rather thanksgiving. For of this you can be sure: No immoral, impure or greedy person--such a man is an idolater--has any inheritance in the kingdom of Christ and of God. Let no one deceive you with empty words, for because of such things God's wrath comes on those who are disobedient. Therefore, do not be partners with them. (Ephesians 5:3-7)

Finally, brothers, whatever is true, whatever is noble, whatever is right, whatever is pure, whatever is lovely, whatever is admirable--if anything is excellent or praiseworthy--think about such things. (Philippians 4:8)

Test everything. Hold on to the good. Avoid every kind of evil. (1 Thessalonians 5:21-22)

Everyone who confesses the name of the Lord must turn away from wickedness. (2 Timothy 2:19)

When tempted, no one should say, "God is tempting me." For God cannot be tempted by evil, nor does he tempt anyone; but each one is tempted when, by his own evil desire, he is dragged away and enticed. Then, after desire has conceived, it gives birth to sin; and sin, when it is full-grown, gives birth to death. (James 1:13-15)

As obedient children, do not conform to the evil desires you had when you lived in ignorance. Peter But just as he who called you is holy, so be holy in all you do; for it is written: "Be holy, because I am holy." (1 Peter 1:14-16)

Be on your guard so that you may not be carried away by the error of lawless men and fall from your secure position. (2 Peter 3:17)

Dear children, do not let anyone lead you astray. (1 John 3:7)

Dear friend, do not imitate what is evil but what is good. Anyone who does what is good is from God. Anyone who does what is evil has not seen God. (3 John 1:11)

CHAPTER SIX

The "it" of Anger

DEFINITION: Anger is an emotional reaction to what you perceive to be a displeasing situation or event, one where you have been offended, wronged, denied, or been a victim of an injustice.

FACTS ABOUT ANGER:

Anger can be positive. Anger is not always wrong. Some anger is good. Positive anger is motivated by unselfishness and is directed against an injustice or wrong behavior. Jesus demonstrated righteous anger in cleansing the temple (Mark 11:15 and 17) and in His response to the Pharisees and their attitudes towards the healing of an infirm man (Mark 3:5).

Improper anger is sin. Improper anger results in aggressive acts of violence, rage, fury, and wrath. Improper anger is sin.

You need help with your anger when you are so angry that you are out of control; when you suppress anger, and redirect it against others or yourself; or when anger results in bitterness, resentment, and hostility.

Mistaken assumptions often lead to anger. You may be angry about something that really didn't happen the way you think or were told it did. You may also make false assumptions about a person's motivation for doing something.

Anger comes from within. You cannot blame your anger on someone else because *".out of the overflow of the heart, his mouth speaks"* (*Luke 6:45*). While you cannot control another's actions, you do have a choice in your own emotional responses

Anger opens the door to other negative attitudes. Anger opens the door for the enemy to come in with other negative emotions and attitudes. *"Do not let the sun go down while you are still angry, and do not give the devil a foothold"* (*Ephesians 4:26-28*). A foothold is "a firm or secure position that provides a base for further advancement" (*American Heritage Dictionary*). If you don't deal with anger in a timely manner, it opens the door to Satan and leads to other negative emotions like resentment, bitterness, and hated. Uncontrolled anger gives birth to more anger.

Anger can kill. Anger affects respiration, blood pressure, the heart, nervous system, and the muscular system. Anger can kill you or cause you to lose control and kill or injure someone else. Anger is not only an emotional and health issue, it is also a spiritual issue.

DEALING WITH ANGER:

Confess anger as sin. Confess improper anger as sin and ask God to forgive you. Take personal responsibility. Do not try to make other people responsible for your anger, i.e., "I have Uncle Harry's temper."

Spend time praying regarding your anger. Make your anger a matter of serious prayer, asking God to help you at the start of each new day. Surrender your emotions to the Holy Spirit. Ask God to remove the roots of anger that are growing inside you. Be on guard, *"Looking diligently lest any man fail of the grace of God; lest any root of bitterness springing up trouble you, and thereby many be defiled" (Hebrews 12:15).* Ask God to change your heart because *"..out of the overflow of the heart, his mouth speaks" (Luke 6:45).*

Analyze the root cause of your anger. What circumstances tend to set you off? Why are you so angry? Is it a learned pattern of response? Destroy the root and kill the fruit.

Practice forgiveness. Unforgiveness is often a root cause anger. Ask God to forgive you, forgive yourself, and then forgive others who have wronged you. As long as you harbor unforgiveness, the person you are angry with is controlling you. Matthew 6:14-15 states: *For if you forgive men when they sin against you, your heavenly Father will also forgive you. But if you do not forgive men their sins, your Father will not forgive your sins.* You may need to confront the person you are angry with by using the steps given in Matthew 18:15-17. Whether the other party repents of wrong or not, you will benefit by knowing you did the right thing

Redirect your anger. Positive directed anger can be a useful tool--for example, anger which motivates a person to strive toward good, like getting laws changed to stop child abuse. Positive anger finds ways to correct wrongs for the good of society. The organization MADD (Mothers Against Drunk Driving) is an example of what can be done with positive anger that is focused on a purpose. If you find yourself becoming angry, ask God to show you ways that your anger can be channeled for good.

Learn how to communicate. Research has proven that when a person is shouted at, he usually shouts back. With patience and practice, you can calm an angry person with your tone of voice. When someone upsets you, calmly talk to them about how you feel. Learn to express yourself better. Don't react before you think. Before speaking, ask yourself if what you are going to say will help or hinder. Ask God to help you remain calm. Expend energy to deal with the problem, not to fuel an emotional response.

Walk away. Remove yourself from the situation or problem until you can respond without anger. Choose to walk away: *Do not set foot on the path of the wicked or walk in the way of evil men. Avoid it, do not travel on it; turn from it and go on your way* (Proverbs 4:14-15).

Do not maintain friendships with angry people. *"Do not make friends with a hot-tempered man, do not associate with one easily angered, or you may learn his ways and get yourself ensnared" (Proverbs 22:24-25).*

Fix your mind on God. Fix your mind on God instead of what is causing your anger: *"You--God--will keep in perfect peace all who trust in you, whose thoughts are fixed on you!" (Isaiah 26:3-4).* Much that you are angry about is temporal with no eternal ramifications.

Think about situations that have caused you anger or that might arouse your anger in the future and pray about how these should be handled.

Immerse yourself in the Word of God. Memorize scriptures concerning anger.

WHAT GOD'S WORD SAYS ABOUT ANGER:

In your anger do not sin. (Psalm 4:4)

Refrain from anger and turn from wrath. (Psalm 37:8)

A quick-tempered man does foolish things. (Proverbs 14:17)

A patient man has great understanding, but a quick-tempered man displays folly. (Proverbs 14:29)

A gentle answer turns away wrath, but a harsh word stirs up anger. (Proverbs 15:1)

A hot-tempered man stirs up dissension, but a patient man calms a quarrel. (Proverbs 15:18)

Do not make friends with a hot-tempered man, do not associate with one easily angered, or you may learn his ways and get yourself ensnared. (Proverbs 22:24-25)

Wise men turn away anger...A fool gives full vent to his anger, but a wise man keeps himself under control. (Proverbs 29:8 and 11)

An angry man stirs up dissension, and a hot-tempered one commits many sins. (Proverbs 29:22)

For as churning the milk produces butter, and as twisting the nose produces blood, so stirring up anger produces strife. (Proverbs 30:33)

Do not be quickly provoked in your spirit, for anger resides in the lap of fools. (Ecclesiastes 7:9)

But I tell you that anyone who is angry with his brother will be subject to judgment... (Matthew 5:22)

In your anger, do not sin. Do not let the sun go down while you are still angry and do not give the devil a foothold. (Ephesians 4:26-27)

You used to walk in these ways, in the life you once lived. But now you must rid yourselves of all such things as these: anger, rage, malice, slander, and filthy language from your lips. (Colossians 3: -8)

I want men everywhere to lift up holy hands in prayer, without anger or disputing. (1 Timothy 2:8)

Make every effort to live in peace with all men. (Hebrews 12:14)

Everyone should be quick to listen, slow to speak and slow to become angry, for man's anger does not bring about the righteous life that God desires. (James 1:19-20)

CHAPTER SEVEN

The "it" of Bitterness

DEFINITION: Bitterness is characterized by an unforgiving spirit and accompanying negative and critical attitudes. It begins when you harbor offences by others, allow disappointments to germinate in your heart, and permit resentment to grow.

FACTS ABOUT BITTERNESS:

Bitterness is destructive. Bitterness is a bottled-up feeling that will eat away at you until you finally explode externally or implode spiritually (Galatians 5:19-20).

Bitterness affects others. Bitterness will spread from you to others: *"See to it that no one misses the grace of God and that no bitter root grows up to cause trouble and defile many"* *(Hebrews 12:15)*

Bitterness affects how you talk. Paul said that the mouths of unrighteous men are filled with "cursing and bitterness" (Romans 3:14).

Bitterness is sin. Peter told a man named Simon: *"You have no part or share in this ministry, because your heart is not right before God. Repent of this wickedness and pray to the Lord. Perhaps he will forgive you for having such a thought in your heart. For I see that you are full of bitterness and captive to sin"* *(Acts 8:20-23).*

Bitterness will hinder your ministry. Peter told Simon that he had no part of the ministry because of the sin and bitterness in his heart.

DEALING WITH BITTERNESS:

Determine what caused your bitterness. What event, circumstance, disappointment, relationship, etc., planted the root of bitterness in your heart? Go to the root cause and identify it so you can deal with it.

Repent of your bitterness. Repent and ask forgiveness for bitterness and the unforgiveness, anger, etc., that caused it.

Extend and ask forgiveness. You may need to ask forgiveness of others who have been affected by your bitter spirit. You may also need to forgive someone who hurt or failed you which led to your bitterness. The Bible commands: *"Get rid of all bitterness, rage and anger, brawling and slander, along with every form of malice. Be kind and compassionate to one another, forgiving each other, just as in Christ God forgave you"* *(Ephesians 4:31-32).*

WHAT GOD'S WORD SAYS ABOUT BITTERNESS:

Hide me from the secret plots of the wicked, From the rebellion of the workers of iniquity,
Who sharpen their tongue like a sword, And bend their bows to shoot their arrows--bitter words,
that they may shoot in secret at the blameless; Suddenly they shoot at him and do not fear.
(Psalm 64:2-4, NKJV)

"You have no part or share in this ministry, because your heart is not right before God. Repent of
this wickedness and pray to the Lord. Perhaps he will forgive you for having such a thought in
your heart. For I see that you are full of bitterness and captive to sin" (Acts 8:20-23).

There is no one righteous, not even one; there is no one who understands, no one who seeks God.
All have turned away, they have together become worthless; there is no one who does good, not
even one. Their throats are open graves; their tongues practice deceit. The poison of vipers is on
their lips. Their mouths are full of cursing and bitterness. Their feet are swift to shed blood; ruin
and misery mark their ways, and the way of peace they do not know.   There is no fear of God
before their eyes.   (Romans 3:10-18)

Love... is not rude, it is not self-seeking, it is not easily angered, it keeps no record of wrongs.
(1 Corinthians 13:5)

Husbands, love your wives and do not be bitter toward them. (Colossians 3:19, NKJV)

Get rid of all bitterness, rage and anger, brawling and slander, along with every form of malice.
Be kind and compassionate to one another, forgiving each other, just as in Christ God forgave
you. (Ephesians 4:31-32)

Follow peace with all men, and holiness, without which no man shall see the Lord. Looking
diligently lest any man fail of the grace of man; lest any root of bitterness springing up trouble
you, and thereby many be defiled. (Hebrews 12:14- 15)

Does a spring send forth fresh water and bitter from the same opening? (James 3:11, NKJV)

But if you have bitter envy and self-seeking in your hearts, do not boast and lie against the truth.
This wisdom does not descend from above, but is earthly, sensual, demonic. (James 3:14-15,
NKJV)

CHAPTER EIGHT

The "it" of Hatred

DEFINITION: Hatred is an intense emotional feeling of hostility towards an individual, a group, or an authority figure in your life.

FACTS ABOUT HATRED:

Hatred is often the root cause of negative emotions like anger, bitterness, rebellion, and hostility.

Hatred never operates in isolation. According to the Word of God, *"hatred stirs up strife" (Proverbs 10:12).* Hatred affects others around you because you become an angry and bitter person.

Hatred is multi-faceted. It affects you spiritually, mentally, emotionally, and physically. Many mental, emotional, and physical maladies have been linked to the negative emotion of hatred.

Hatred usually involves a refusal to forgive someone.

Hatred is sin. The Bible states that if you hate your brother, you are in spiritual darkness (1 John 2 :9). God compares hatred to murder (1 John 3:15).

You cannot love God and hate someone. The Bible declares: *"If anyone says, "I love God," yet hates his brother, he is a liar. For anyone who does not love his brother, whom he has seen, cannot love God, whom he has not seen" (1 John 4:20).*

DEALING WITH HATRED:

Confess hatred as sin. That is what it is, according to the Bible. Ask God to forgive you.

Forgive the one who offended you. You may need to confront the person and ask for or extend forgiveness. You must resolve the root causes behind your hatred.

Pray for your enemy and extend mercy. Luke 6:27-36 directs you to pray for your enemies, respond to their needs, and extend to them the same mercy that a merciful God has extended to you.

Keep your heart from hatred. Do not allow bitterness and unforgiveness to fester into hatred. *"Keep your heart with all diligence, for out of it spring the issues of life" (Proverbs 4:23, NKJV) You* "keep your heart" through prayer and study and application of God's Word.

Ask God to release love to replace the hatred. Study 1 Corinthians 13 and ask God to develop in your life the qualities of love listed there.

WHAT GOD'S WORD SAYS ABOUT HATRED:

Do not hate your brother in your heart. (Leviticus 19:17)

Do not drag me away with the wicked, with those who do evil, who speak cordially with their neighbors but harbor malice in their hearts. (Psalm 28:3)

Hatred stirs up dissension, but love covers over all wrongs. (Proverbs 10:12)

You have heard that it was said, "Love your neighbor and hate your enemy." But I tell you: Love your enemies and pray for those who persecute you, that you may be sons of your Father in heaven. (Matthew 5:43-44)

But I tell you who hear me: Love your enemies, do good to those who hate you, bless those who curse you, pray for those who mistreat you. If someone strikes you on one cheek, turn to him the other also. If someone takes your cloak, do not stop him from taking your tunic. Give to everyone who asks you, and if anyone takes what belongs to you, do not demand it back. Do to others as you would have them do to you. If you love those who love you, what credit is that to you? Even 'sinners' love those who love them. And if you do good to those who are good to you, what credit is that to you? Even 'sinners' do that. And if you lend to those from whom you expect repayment, what credit is that to you? Even 'sinners' lend to 'sinners,' expecting to be repaid in full. But love your enemies, do good to them, and lend to them without expecting to get anything back. Then your reward will be great, and you will be sons of the Most High, because he is kind to the ungrateful and wicked. Be merciful, just as your Father is merciful. (Luke 6:27-36)

If your brother sins, rebuke him, and if he repents, forgive him. (Luke 17:3)

The acts of the sinful nature are obvious: sexual immorality, impurity and debauchery; idolatry and witchcraft; hatred, discord, jealousy, fits of rage, selfish ambition, dissensions, factions and envy; drunkenness, orgies, and the like. I warn you, as I did before, that those who live like this will not inherit the kingdom of God. (Galatians 5:19-21)

Get rid of all bitterness, rage and anger, brawling and slander, along with every form of malice. (Ephesians 4:31)

Therefore, rid yourselves of all malice and all deceit, hypocrisy, envy and slander of every kind. (1 Peter 2:1)

Anyone who claims to be in the light but hates his brother is still in the darkness. Whoever loves his brother lives in the light, and there is nothing in him to make him stumble. But whoever hates his brother is in the darkness and walks around in the darkness; he does not know where he is going, because the darkness has blinded him. (1 John 2:9-11)

Anyone who hates his brother is a murderer, and you know that no murderer has eternal life in him. (1 John 3:15)

If anyone says, "I love God," yet hates his brother, he is a liar. For anyone who does not love his brother, whom he has seen, cannot love God, whom he has not seen. And he has given us this command: Whoever loves God must also love his brother. (1 John 4:20-21)

CHAPTER NINE

The "it" of Lying

DEFINITION: A lie is a statement that deviates from or perverts the truth. It is also called bearing false witness in the Bible.

FACTS ABOUT LYING:

Satan is the father of lies. This means all lies are instigated by satanic or demonic influences (John 8:44).

Lying is sin. Leviticus 19:11 declares: *"Do not lie. Do not deceive one another" (Leviticus 19:11).*

Lying is one of the main sins God hates. See Proverbs 6:16-19.

Lying begins in your heart. *"For out of the heart come evil thoughts, murder, adultery, sexual immorality, theft, false testimony, slander" (Matthew 15:19).*

Lying can become compulsive. Lying can become a deeply ingrained habit and you can eventually become what is known as a "pathological liar"--you lie about everything.

DEALING WITH LYING:

Ask God to forgive you. Lying is sin, and as with all sins, forgiveness from God must be sought.

Ask forgiveness of others. Seek forgiveness from the ones you lied to or about. If you lied about finances or your lie resulted in any type of losses for someone, make restitution.

Bind the spirit of lying. In the name of Jesus, bind the demonic spirit of lying from operating in your life. Loose the Spirit of Truth to operate.

WHAT GOD'S WORD SAYS ABOUT LYING:

You shall not give false testimony against your neighbor. (Exodus 20:16)

Do not lie. Do not deceive one another. (Leviticus 19:11)

You shall not give false testimony against your neighbor. (Deuteronomy 5:20)

You destroy those who tell lies; bloodthirsty and deceitful men the Lord abhors. (Psalm 5:6)

Whoever of you loves life and desires to see many good days, keep your tongue from evil and your lips from speaking lies. (Psalm 34:12-13)

You love evil rather than good, falsehood rather than speaking the truth. (Psalm 52:3)

No one who practices deceit will dwell in my house; no one who speaks falsely will stand in my presence. (Psalm 101:7)

I hate and abhor falsehood but I love your law. (Psalm 119:163)

There are six things the Lord hates, seven that are detestable to him: haughty eyes, a lying tongue, hands that shed innocent blood, a heart that devises wicked schemes, feet that are quick to rush into evil, a false witness who pours out lies and a man who stirs up dissension among brothers. (Proverbs 6:16-19)

The integrity of the upright guides them, but the unfaithful are destroyed by their duplicity. (Proverbs 11:3)

Truthful lips endure forever, but a lying tongue lasts only a moment. (Proverbs 12:19)

The Lord detests lying lips, but he delights in men who are truthful. (Proverbs 12:22)

The righteous hate what is false, but the wicked bring shame and disgrace. (Proverbs 13:5)

He whose tongue is deceitful falls into trouble. (Proverbs 17:20)

Better to be poor than a liar. (Proverbs 19:22)

An honest answer is like a kiss on the lips. (Proverbs 24:26)

Keep me from deceitful ways; be gracious to me through your law. (Psalm 119:29)

Like a club or a sword or a sharp arrow is the man who gives false testimony against his neighbor. (Proverbs 25:18)

Like a madman shooting firebrands or deadly arrows is a man who deceives his neighbor and says, "I was only joking!" (Proverbs 26:18-19)

A lying tongue hates those it hurts, and a flattering mouth works ruin. (Proverbs 26:28)

Keep falsehood and lies far from me. (Proverbs 30:7-8)

O Lord, do not your eyes look for truth? (Jeremiah 5:3)

Friend deceives friend, and no one speaks the truth. They have taught their tongues to lie; they weary themselves with sinning. (Jeremiah 9:5)

For by your words you will be acquitted, and by your words you will be condemned. (Matthew 12:37)

For out of the heart come evil thoughts, murder, adultery, sexual immorality, theft, false testimony, slander. (Matthew 15:19)

"You know the commandments: 'Do not commit adultery, do not murder, do not steal, do not give false testimony, honor your father and mother.'" (Luke 18:20)

You belong to your father, the devil, and you want to carry out your father's desire. He was a murderer from the beginning, not holding to the truth, for there is no truth in him. When he lies, he speaks his native language, for he is a liar and the father of lies. (John 8:44)

For the commandments, "You shall not commit adultery, you shall not murder, you shall not steal, you shall not bear false witness, you shall not covet," and if there is any other commandment, are all summed up in this saying, namely, "You shall love your neighbor as yourself." Love does no harm to a neighbor; therefore, love is the fulfillment of the law. (Romans 13:9-10)

Therefore, each of you must put off falsehood and speak truthfully to his neighbor, for we are all members of one body. (Ephesians 4:25)

Do not lie to each other, since you have taken off your old self with its practices and have put on the new self, which is being renewed in knowledge in the image of its Creator. (Colossians 3:9-10)

CHAPTER TEN

The "it" of Profanity

DEFINITION: Profanity is language or behavior that shows disrespect for God, Jesus, or the Holy Spirit including misuse of their names. It is vulgar and irreverent language or behavior, including jokes or innuendos that mock that which is holy.

FACTS ABOUT PROFANITY:

Your words are powerful. The Bible says that death and life are in your words (Proverbs 18:21). When you use profanity, you are speaking words of death because profanity is sin and God will judge it.

The tongue is unruly. It is compared to a fire (James 3:5); a burning fire (Proverbs 16:27); a world of iniquity (James 3:6); a beast that needs taming (James 3:7-8); a fountain of either fresh or bitter water (James 3:11); a tree bearing either good or evil fruit (James 3:12); an unruly evil (James 3:8); deadly poison (James 3:8); a sharp razor (Psalms 52:2); a sharp sword (Psalms 57:4; 59:7); a poisonous serpent (Psalms 140:3); a deep pit (Proverbs 22:14).

What you speak comes from your heart. Profane words come from your own heart--not because someone made you angry or because you learned the words from your parents or friends. (Matthew 12:34).

Profanity is sin. The Bible declares: *"You shall not misuse the name of the Lord your God, for the Lord will not hold anyone guiltless who misuses his name" (Exodus 20:7).*

DEALING WITH PROFANITY:

Recognize your mouth is your responsibility. You will give account for every word you speak, including profanity that takes the name of God and holy things in vain. (Matthew 12:36-37)

Ask God to forgive you. Profanity is sin and, as in the case of all sin, requires confession and repentance.

Ask God to change your heart. The words you speak come from your heart, so you need a change of heart (Matthew 15:18-20).

Ask God to guard your words. David said: *"...I have resolved that my mouth will not sin" (Psalm 17:3b).*

Think before you speak. Proverbs says to clap your hand over your mouth if necessary (Proverbs 15:28).

Separate yourself from those who cannot control their tongues. The Bible says to *"Stay away from a foolish man, for you will not find knowledge on his lips" (Proverbs 14:7).* Do not hang out with them and allow them to pour their filthy, godless, profane words into your spirit.

Excuse yourself when others are using profanity. If they ask why you are leaving, tell them! If they are bold enough to use that kind of language, you should be bold enough to confront it.

WHAT GOD'S WORD SAYS ABOUT PROFANITY:

You shall not misuse the name of the Lord your God, for the Lord will not hold anyone guiltless who misuses his name. (Exodus 20:7)

...I have resolved that my mouth will not sin. (Psalm 17:3b)

I said, "I will watch my ways and keep my tongue from sin; I will put a muzzle on my mouth. " (Psalm 39:1-2a)

They speak of you with evil intent; your adversaries misuse your name. (Psalm 139:20)

Put away perversity from your mouth; keep corrupt talk far from your lips. (Proverbs 4:24)

The lips of the righteous know what is fitting, but the mouth of the wicked only what is perverse. (Proverbs 10:32)

The heart of the righteous weighs its answers, but the mouth of the wicked gushes evil. (Proverbs 15:28)

The tongue has the power of life and death... (Proverbs 18:21)

Better a poor man whose walk is blameless than a fool whose lips are perverse. (Proverbs 19:1)

Like a fluttering sparrow or a darting swallow, an undeserved curse does not come to rest. (Proverbs 26:2)

Do not let your mouth lead you into sin. (Ecclesiastes 5:6)

But I tell you that men will have to give account on the day of judgment for every careless word they have spoken. For by your words you will be acquitted, and by your words you will be condemned. (Matthew 12:36-37)

But the things that come out of the mouth come from the heart, and these make a man 'unclean.' For out of the heart come evil thoughts, murder, adultery, sexual immorality, theft, false testimony, slander. (Matthew 15:18-19)

Do not let any unwholesome talk come out of your mouths, but only what is helpful for building others up according to their needs, that it may benefit those who listen. (Ephesians 4:29)

Nor should there be obscenity, foolish talk or coarse joking, which are out of place, but rather thanksgiving. (Ephesians 5:4)

But now you must rid yourselves of all such things as these: anger, rage, malice, slander, and filthy language from your lips. (Colossians 3:8)

If anyone considers himself religious and yet does not keep a tight rein on his tongue, he deceives himself and his religion is worthless. (James 1:26)

But just as he who called you is holy, so be holy in all you do... (1 Peter 1:15)

Whoever would love life and see good days must keep his tongue from evil and his lips from deceitful speech. (1 Peter 3:10)

CHAPTER ELEVEN

The "it" of Gossip

DEFINITION: Gossip is sharing private information with those who are not part of the circumstances, problem, or solution. It includes idle talk, spreading rumors, or outright slander about someone.

FACTS ABOUT GOSSIP:

Gossip is not limited to spreading information. It includes improper involvement in another person's affairs--what the Bible calls busybodies (1 Timothy 5:13). Gossip is spreading rumors and making false accusations about someone, and it causes division and confusion.

Gossip is sin. The Bible commands: *"You shall not go about as a talebearer among your people; nor shall you take a stand against the life of your neighbor: I am the Lord" (Leviticus 19:16, NKJV).*

Associating with a person who gossips is sin. The Bible says: *"He who goes about as a talebearer reveals secrets; therefore, associate not with him who talks too freely" (Proverbs 20:19, AMP)*

Your tongue is unruly. It is compared to a fire (James 3:5); a burning fire (Proverbs 16:27); a world of iniquity (James 3:6); a beast that needs taming (James 3:7-8); a fountain of either fresh or bitter water (James 3:11); a tree bearing either good or evil fruit (James 3:12); an unruly evil (James 3:8); deadly poison (James 3:8); a sharp razor (Psalms 52:2); a sharp sword (Psalms 57:4; 59:7); a poisonous serpent (Psalms 140:3); a deep pit (Proverbs 22:14).

DEALING WITH GOSSIP:

Repent of the sin of gossip. Whether you have been spreading gossip or listening to it, ask God to forgive you.

Ask God to set a watch before your mouth. Pray the prayer of the psalmist: *"Set a guard over my mouth, O Lord; keep watch over the door of my lips" (Psalm 141:3).*

Ask forgiveness of anyone whose reputation has been harmed by the gossip you have spread.

In the future, before speaking, ask these questions:
    -Will what I am about to say bring glory to God?
    -Is it the truth?
    -Is it fair to all concerned?
    -Will it be beneficial to all concerned?
    -Will it edify others?
    -Have I talked to the person I am talking about?
    -Is what I am saying a fact that needs to be shared or is it based on rumors and does not

need to be said?
-Is it absolutely necessary that I share this?

Separate yourself from those who gossip. *"Stay away from a foolish man, for you will not find knowledge on his lips" (Proverbs 14:7).* Do not hang out with them and allow them to pour their tidbits of gossip into your spirit. *"A gossip betrays a confidence; so, avoid a man who talks too much" (Proverbs 20:19).* The Bible says to warn a divisive person, then separate from them if they do not listen (Titus 3:10-11).

WHAT GOD'S WORD SAYS ABOUT GOSSIP:

You shall not give false testimony against your neighbor. (Exodus 20:16)

Do not spread false reports. Do not help a wicked man by being a malicious witness. (Exodus 23:1)

Do not go about spreading slander among your people. (Leviticus 19:16)

Not a word from their mouth can be trusted; their heart is filled with destruction. Their throat is an open grave; with their tongue they speak deceit. (Psalm 5:9)

Reckless words pierce like a sword, but the tongue of the wise brings healing. (Proverbs 12:18)

The tongue of the wise commends knowledge, but the mouth of the fool gushes folly. (Proverbs 15:2)

A perverse man stirs up dissension, and a gossip separates close friends. (Proverbs 16:28)

He who covers over an offense promotes love, but whoever repeats the matter separates close friends. (Proverbs 17:9)

A man of knowledge uses words with restraint, and a man of understanding is even-tempered. Even a fool is thought wise if he keeps silent, and discerning if he holds his tongue. (Proverbs 17:27-28)

The words of a gossip are like choice morsels; they go down to a man's inmost parts. (Proverbs 18:8)

Let the words of my mouth, and the meditation of my heart, be acceptable in thy sight, O Lord, my strength, and my redeemer. (Psalms 19:14, KJV)

He that goeth about as a tale-bearer revealeth secrets; Therefore, company not with him that openeth wide his lips. (Proverbs 20:19 NAS)

Keep your tongue from evil and your lips from speaking lies. (Psalms 34:13)

I said, I will take heed to my ways, that I sin not with my tongue: I will keep my mouth with a bridle, while the wicked is before me. (Psalms 39:1, KJV)

My enemies say of me in malice, "When will he die and his name perish?" Whenever one comes to see me, he speaks falsely, while his heart gathers slander; then he goes out and spreads it abroad. (Psalm 41:5-6)

You love every harmful word, Oh you deceitful tongue! (Psalm 52:4)

Whoever slanders his neighbor in secret, him will I put to silence. (Psalm 101:5)

Set a guard over my mouth, O Lord; keep watch over the door of my lips. (Psalm 141:3)

Put away perversity from your mouth; keep corrupt talk far from your lips. (Proverbs 4:24)

Hear; For I will speak of excellent things; and the opening of my lips shall be right things. For my mouth shall speak truth; and wickedness is an abomination to my lips. All the words of my mouth are in righteousness; there is nothing froward or perverse in them. (Proverbs 8:6-8, KJV)

...Whoever spreads slander is a fool. (Proverbs 10:18)

With his mouth the godless destroys his neighbor, but through knowledge the righteous escape. (Proverbs 11:9)

A gossip betrays a confidence, but a trustworthy man keeps a secret. (Proverbs 11:13)

A perverse man stirs up dissension, and a gossip separates close friends. (Proverbs 16:28)

A wicked man listens to evil lips; a liar pays attention to malicious tongue. (Proverbs 17:4)

He who covers over an offense promotes love, but whoever repeats the matter separates close friends. (Proverbs 17:9)

A gossip betrays a confidence; so, avoid a man who talks too much. (Proverbs 20:19)

The words of a gossip are like choice morsels; they go down to a man's inmost parts. (Proverbs 18:8)

The mouth of the wicked gulps down evil. (Proverbs 19:28)

A gossip betrays a confidence; so, avoid a man who talks too much. (Proverbs 20:19)

Without wood a fire goes out; without gossip a quarrel dies down. (Proverbs 26:20)

Do not let your mouth lead you into sin... (Ecclesiastes 5:6)

Do not pay attention to every word people say. (Ecclesiastes 7:21)

Their tongue is a deadly arrow; it speaks with deceit. With his mouth each speaks cordially to his neighbor, but in his heart, he sets a trap for him. (Jeremiah 9:8)

Men will have to give account on the day of judgment for every careless word they have spoken. For by your words you will be acquitted, and by your words you will be condemned. (Matthew 12:36-37)

Furthermore, since they did not think it worthwhile to retain the knowledge of God, he gave them over to a depraved mind, to do what ought not to be done. They have become filled with every kind of wickedness, evil, greed and depravity. They are full of envy, murder, strife, deceit and malice. They are gossips, slanderers, God-haters, insolent, arrogant and boastful; they invent ways of doing evil; they disobey their parents; they are senseless, faithless, heartless, ruthless. Although they know God's righteous decree that those who do such things deserve death, they not only continue to do these very things but also approve of those who practice them. (Romans 1:29-30)

You, therefore, have no excuse, you who pass judgment on someone else, for at whatever point you judge the other, you are condemning yourself, because you who pass judgment do the same things (Romans 2:1)

The poison of vipers is on their lips. Their mouths are full of cursing and bitterness. (Romans 3:13-14)

For I fear lest, when I come, I shall not find you such as I wish, and that I shall be found by you such as you do not wish; lest there be contentions, jealousies, outbursts of wrath, selfish ambitions, backbitings, whisperings, conceits, tumults. (2 Corinthians 12:20, NKJV)

Let no corrupt communication proceed out of your mouth, but that which is good to the use of edifying, that it may minister grace unto the hearers. (Ephesians 4:29, KJV)

Let all...evil speaking be put away from you... (Ephesians 4:31, KJV)

But now also put off...filthy communication out of your mouth. (Colossians 3:8, NKJV)

And whatever you do, whether in word or deed, do it all in the name of the Lord Jesus, giving thanks to God the Father through him. (Colossians 3:17)

Don't let anyone look down on you because you are young, but set an example for the believers in speech, in life, in love, in faith and in purity. (1 Timothy 4:12)

And not only do they become idlers, but also gossips and busybodies, saying things they ought not to. (1 Timothy 5:13)

Remind the people to be subject to rulers and authorities, to be obedient, to be ready to do whatever is good, to slander no one, to be peaceable and considerate, and to show true humility toward all men. (Titus 3:1-2)

Warn a divisive person once, and then warn him a second time. After that, have nothing to do with him. You may be sure that such a man is warped and sinful; he is self-condemned. (Titus 3:10-11)

Brothers, do not slander one another. Anyone who speaks against his brother or judges him speaks against the law and judges it. When you judge the law, you are not keeping it, but sitting in judgment on it. There is only one Lawgiver and Judge, the one who is able to save and destroy. But you--who are you to judge your neighbor? (James 4:11)

...be holy in all manner of conversation; Because it is written, be holy; for I am holy. (1 Peter 1:15-16)

Whoever would love life and see good days must keep his tongue from evil and his lips from deceitful speech. (I Peter 3:10)

CHAPTER TWELVE

The "it" of Murder

DEFINITION: To murder is to take the life of another with willful malice and forethought.

FACTS ABOUT MURDER:

Murder is sin. One of the ten commandments given by God was, *"You shall not murder"* *(Exodus 20:13)*. Murder is sin, but it is not the unpardonable sin. You can be forgiven by God.

Murder begins in the heart. *"For out of the heart come evil thoughts, murder, adultery, sexual immorality, theft, false testimony, slander" (Matthew 15:19)*. Murder is a work of the flesh--the old sinful nature (Galatians 5:19-21).

Murder is not the same as self-defense or an accidental killing. Self-defense is permitted by the laws of most governments. People who killed someone accidentally in Bible times were protected from penalties.

Abortion of an unborn child is murder. It is the termination of the life of a human being. An unborn child is a living soul from the moment of conception (Jeremiah 1:5; Psalm 139:13-16). (See the topic of "Abortion" in this database.)

Murder affects more than the person who was killed. The loss of a life is most tragic, of course, but the friends and family of the one murdered and the one doing the killing are also tragically affected by this sinful act.

The New Testament definition of murder was expanded to include anyone who hates another person: John wrote: *"Anyone who hates his brother is a murderer, and you know that no murderer has eternal life in him" (1 John 3:15)*. You may not have actually murdered someone physically, but you are considered a murderer if you hate someone. The New Testament also makes it clear that if you offend in one sin, you are guilty of all (James 2:10-11).

DEALING WITH MURDER:

Ask God for forgiveness. Murder is sin and, as with all sin, you must confess it to God and ask forgiveness. If you have not physically harmed someone but you hate them, you should seek forgiveness for your hatred which, in the New Testament, is equated with murder. These things are works of the flesh--the old sinful nature--and if you continue in them without seeking forgiveness, you will not inherit the Kingdom of God.

Ask friends and family for forgiveness. Ask forgiveness of the friends and family of the one you killed. Ask forgiveness of your own friends and family for the tragic circumstances which you put them through.

Make restitution. You will most likely be required to make legal restitution by serving time in prison and you may also make restitution by providing financially for the victim's family.

Forgive yourself. Do not live under the shadow of shame. Although murder is a terrible crime, your sin is forgiven and Jesus bore both your sin and the shame of it on the cross (Hebrews 12:2).

If you are a friend or family member of a murder victim, you must forgive the one who murdered your loved one. The biblical concept of forgiveness is not just for the minor offences in life, but also for the major tragedies that affect our lives.

WHAT GOD'S WORD SAYS ABOUT MURDER:

You shall not murder. (Exodus 20:13)

For you created my inmost being; you knit me together in my mother's womb. I praise you because I am fearfully and wonderfully made; your works are wonderful, I know that full well. All the days ordained for me were written in your book before one of them came to be. My frame was not hidden from you when I was made in the secret place. When I was woven together in the depths of the earth, your eyes saw my unformed body (Psalm 139:13-16)

This is what the Lord says - he who made you, who formed you in the womb. (Isaiah 44:2)

"Before I formed you in the womb I knew you, before you were born I set you apart..." (Jeremiah 1:5)

You have heard that it was said to the people long ago, 'Do not murder, and anyone who murders will be subject to judgment.' But I tell you that anyone who is angry with his brother will be subject to judgment... (Matthew 5:21-22)

"You have heard that it was said, 'Eye for eye, and tooth for tooth.' But I tell you, do not resist an evil person. If someone strikes you on the right cheek, turn to him the other also. And if someone wants to sue you and take your tunic, let him have your cloak as well. If someone forces you to go one mile, go with him two miles. Give to the one who asks you, and do not turn away from the one who wants to borrow from you. You have heard that it was said, 'Love your neighbor and hate your enemy.' But I tell you: Love your enemies and pray for those who persecute you, that you may be sons of your Father in heaven. He causes his sun to rise on the evil and the good, and sends rain on the righteous and the unrighteous. If you love those who love you, what reward will you get? Are not even the tax collectors doing that? And if you greet only your brothers, what are you doing more than others? Do not even pagans do that? Be perfect, therefore, as your heavenly Father is perfect." (Matthew 5:38-48)

For out of the heart come evil thoughts, murder, adultery, sexual immorality, theft, false testimony, slander. (Matthew 15:19)

Jesus replied, "'Do not murder...'" (Matthew 19:18)
They have become filled with every kind of wickedness, evil, greed and depravity. They are full of envy, murder, strife, deceit and malice. (Romans 1:29)

Do not take revenge, my friends, but leave room for God's wrath, for it is written: "It is mine to avenge; I will repay," says the Lord. On the contrary: "If your enemy is hungry, feed him; if he is thirsty, give him something to drink. In doing this, you will heap burning coals on his head." Do not be overcome by evil, but overcome evil with good. (Romans 12:19-21)

The commandments, "Do not commit adultery," "Do not murder," "Do not steal," "Do not covet," and whatever another commandment there may be, are summed up in this one rule: "Love your neighbor as yourself." (Romans 13:9)

The acts of the sinful nature are obvious: sexual immorality, impurity and debauchery; idolatry and witchcraft; hatred, discord, jealousy, fits of rage, selfish ambition, dissensions, factions and envy; drunkenness, orgies, and the like. I warn you, as I did before, that those who live like this will not inherit the kingdom of God. (Galatians 5:19-21)

For he who said, "Do not commit adultery," also said, "Do not murder." If you do not commit adultery but do commit murder, you have become a lawbreaker. (James 2:10-11)

You want something but don't get it. You kill and covet, but you cannot have what you want. You quarrel and fight. You do not have, because you do not ask God. When you ask, you do not receive, because you ask with wrong motives, that you may spend what you get on your pleasures. (James 4:2-3)

If you suffer, it should not be as a murderer or thief or any other kind of criminal, or even as a meddler. (1 Peter 4:15)

Anyone who hates his brother is a murderer, and you know that no murderer has eternal life in him. (1 John 3:15)

But the cowardly, the unbelieving, the vile, the murderers, the sexually immoral, those who practice magic arts, the idolaters and all liars--their place will be in the fiery lake of burning sulfur. This is the second death. (Revelation 21:8)

CONCLUSION

How to Get Rid of "it" though Personal Deliverance

When you understand self-deliverance, you will keep yourself from being bond; you will keep yourself healthy, physically and spiritually and be free from spiritual pollution. Every day, you will enjoy divine health and will not be spending your money on drugs and hospital bills.

Sometimes, there may not be a minister who is anointed and knowledgeable about deliverance to help you. Sometimes, you can be heavily attacked and the next service is about four days away. What do you do? You should never allow evil spirits to reside in your life. If you lack adequate time to do a self-deliverance in the mornings, after your quiet time, then, when you're having your bath, you could do it.

Whatever the causes of our spiritual afflictions, there are several proven steps we may try to help ourselves find freedom and healing. If these steps do not resolve your situation, then perhaps it is time to ask for help:

Step 1 — Conversion

Deliverance from any level of bondage, or harassment (collectively called, "spiritual afflictions") cannot be achieved without personal conversion. Deliverance from milder forms of spiritual affliction may often be achieved by the various acts of personal conversion—Acts of Contrition, Faith, Hope, Charity, and Consecration. "Prayer Acts" and other prayers, with fasting, and various devotions are often effective to drive evil spirits away:

So humble yourselves before God. Resist the Devil, and he will flee from you. Draw close to God, and God will draw close to you. — (James 4:7,8)

The first step, therefore, is make up your mind to live the Christ-life; or if already doing so, to persevere in living the Christ-life. This internal conversion, which is a conscious decision and determination to follow Christ and all of His teachings, precedes all other steps to deliverance. Without conversion to the Faith in Jesus Christ and participation in His family, the Church, deliverance, even if seemingly effective for a while, cannot be successful in the long run. It is the *"Truth"* that makes us free (John 8:31b), not prayers, rituals, counseling, or personal will in themselves. It is the confrontation with Truth that sends the demons running back to hell. This is why the method of Deliverance Counseling we use is called a *"Truth Encounter"*. As demons are confronted with the Truth, and as we are confronted with the Truth, of whom we are in Christ, we gain freedom. The foundation of all truth is Jesus Christ, who is Truth (John 14:6). Without our Lord Jesus Christ, we can never know truth or obtain it.

Some people believe they are unable to make a profession of faith in Jesus Christ. In such cases the person should ask God for help—ask Him for the faith that will save, deliver, and heal.

If we are willing to accept the gift of faith from God, our Lord will give it to us when we ask:

And I tell you, Ask, and it will be given you; seek, and you will find; knock, and it will be opened to you. For every one who asks receives, and he who seeks finds, and to him who knocks it will be opened. What father among you, if his son asks for a fish, will instead of a fish give him a serpent; or if he asks for an egg, will give him a scorpion? If you then, who are evil, know how to give good gifts to your children, how much more will the heavenly Father give the Holy Spirit to those who ask him! — (Luke 11:9-13)

Sincerely ask God for the faith that brings saving faith, the faith of conversion to the One, that is Jesus Christ, whom who declares:

I am the way, and the truth, and the life; no one comes to the Father, but by me (John 14:6) .... Come to me, all who labor and are heavy laden, and I will give you rest (Matthew 11:28) .... I will not reject anyone who comes to me (John 6:37) .... [rather] take my yoke upon you, and learn from me; for I am gentle and lowly in heart, and you will find rest for your souls. For my yoke is easy, and my burden is light (Matt 11:29-30)

Step 2 — Repentance

Essential to growing closer to God in faith, devotion, and love is to repent of those behaviors, desires, beliefs, and ideas that are sinful. The definition of sin is much broader than most people imagine. A definition of sin:

Sin is an offense against reason, truth, and right conscience; it is a failure in genuine love for God and neighbor caused by a perverse attachment to certain goods. Its wounds the nature of man and injures human solidarity. It has been defined as "an utterance, a deed, or a desire contrary to the eternal law."

Sin is an offense against God: *"Against you, you alone, have I sinned, and done that which is evil in your sight"* (Ps 51:4). Sin sets itself against God's love for us and turns our hearts away from it. Like the first sin (of Adam and Eve), it is disobedience, a revolt against God through the will to become "like gods" (Gen 3:5), knowing and determining good and evil. Sin is thus "love of oneself even to contempt of God." In this proud self-exaltation, sin is diametrically opposed to the obedience of Jesus, which achieves our salvation (cf. Phil 2:6-9).

We must repent of our sin, but repentance involves more than merely "turning away" from sin. Repentance must also renounce all that opposes God and all that He finds sinful. This includes renouncing Satan and his ways, renouncing personal sins, and renouncing all that leads us to sin. Some of the common sins and situations that interfere with deliverance include: involvement in non-Christian activities like the occult; persistent situational sins such as living together without marriage or remarriage without annulment of previous marriages; maintaining improper or problematic friendships; illegal activities of any sort; and sins that have become habitual such as pornography, masturbation, fornication, gossip, lying, stealing, etc.

The three greatest stumbling blocks to deliverance is Pride, Rebellion, and Unforgiveness and all the things that go along with those three sins. Repentance of Pride, Rebellion, and Unforgiveness is required to even hope for deliverance. Repentance also includes the firm amendment to avoid sin, and the near occasion of sin, in the future. Repentance requires a *complete* turnaround of our lives, a becoming a *"new man"*, so that...

...you should put away the old self of your former way of life, corrupted through deceitful desires, and be renewed in the spirit of your minds, and put on the new self, created in God's way in righteousness and holiness of truth. Therefore, putting away falsehood, speak the truth, each one to his neighbor, for we are members one of another...(thus) do not leave room for the devil (Eph 4:22-25,26b)

Step 3 — Confession

With faith and contrition of heart, repentance of mind, firm purpose to avoid sin and that which leads us to sin, we must now confess our sins before our God who is a God of forgiveness and mercy. This is a critical step that we will discuss at length.

The manner of our confession differs, but within our respective traditions, confession is required:

If we confess our sins, he is faithful and just, and will forgive our sins and cleanse us from all unrighteousness. (1 John 1:9)

... if you confess with your mouth that Jesus is Lord and believe in your heart that God raised him from the dead, you will be saved. For one believes with the heart and so is justified, and one confesses with the mouth and so is saved. (Romans 10:9-10)

"Confess your sins to each other and pray for each other so that you may be healed. The earnest prayer of a righteous person has great power and wonderful results" (James 5:16).

This confidant maybe one's pastor or another minister, or a trusted friend. We must be careful when choosing an "accountability partner." Since we will be revealing very private and sensitive information about ourselves, it is critically important to trust whoever we choose as a confidant to be discreet and to keep absolutely confidential the information we tell them.

There is wisdom in presenting oneself to an "accountability partner." Personal accountability is upheld when we confess to another person whom may hold us accountable for our actions. Confessing our sins to one another is a powerful way to break the bonds of sin in our lives. It is much harder to confess our sins to one another than to simply say, *"Lord, forgive me"*. While God is forgiving, of course, it is the demands of personal accountability before another human being that brings our confession into grounded reality that strengthens our commitment to turn away from sin in the future.

Religious ministers, psychologists, counselors, and others including the Deliverance Counselors of agency, are also bound either by law, ethical codes, or contract with the client (or bound by any combination thereof) to keep private and confidential all that is revealed to them. In addition, those in the ministerial and helping professions are usually trained in the ethics, legalities, and culture of maintaining confidentiality. They are use to keeping private the personal information of their patients and clients. Friends, on the other hand, may not have such training and may not be use to the culture of confidentiality. Thus, if one's confidant is not a pastor, or at least a minister, psychologist, or counselor bound by law and/or ethical codes, take care to ensure the chosen confidant understands thoroughly that he must keep private all that he hears and may not discuss it with anyone, not even with his spouse.

There is a great psychological comfort in hearing the words, "I forgive you" or the equivalent, "I absolve you of your sins." Our Father in heaven understands this psychological need. Thus, in His great love for us, He provided a way for us to hear those words in His name. It is God who ultimately forgives sins, but God, according to His sovereign authority chose to delegate this authority to His validly ordained priests. This power was given to the Apostles in John 20:22-23 and was passed on from them to those whom they appointed.

Our Father in heaven also knows and understands our need to be a family and for the family to come to our aid when we are hurting, to offer forgiveness when we fall, and to provide healing and strength to help us grow in faith. God forgives you when you appeal to Him with your heart-felt and sincere repentance and confession. Follow the tradition of your denomination and always offer a prayer for forgiveness as soon as possible after sinning. Then, in obedience to the Bible, seek accountability by confession to a confidant to complete your healing.

Step 4 — Removing the Greatest Stumbling blocks: Pride, Rebellion, and Forgiveness

We have already mentioned that the three biggest stumbling blocks to deliverance is usually Pride, Rebellion, and Unforgiveness. These three sins distance us from God. To draw closer to God we need to give up our pride, obey our Lord's teachings, and forgive those who hurt us.

In Deliverance Counseling we help our clients through exercises to locate pockets of pride and rebellion and to rid themselves of these sins with the help of God through prayer. Forgiveness, however, tends to be the most difficult, partly because of pride or even rebellion perhaps, but mostly because of deeply emotional issues surrounding the circumstances of the hurts someone has given us. Whatever the causes of our unforgiveness, deliverance is not possible until we can come to forgive, thus we shall discuss this topic at some length too.

The following guide is rather long, but this step is one of the most important. One simple MUST deals with Pride, Rebellion, and Unforgiveness if deliverance and healing is to be permanently possible.

Pride: Pride is the essential sin that leads to most other sins. It is the sin of Lucifer that led him to rebel against God resulting in his expulsion from heaven and becoming Satan.

Pride is a killer. Pride says, "I can do it! I can get myself out of this mess without God and without anyone else's helped." No, we can't! We absolutely need God, and we desperately need each other.

Pride also says "I know the best and most efficient way and how dare others get in the way of that" or "How dare things not go my way" or "How dare some person or something get in the way of what I want to do." Impatience is a factor of pride. Other ways impatience reveals our pride is getting impatient when we cannot find our car keys, or when we are late to a meeting, or if someone is driving too slowly for us on the hi-way, or when the computer acts up and interrupts our train of thought.

Impatience is the sister to Pride because it is caused essentially by our desire to have things our own way, in our own time, and according to our own preferences.

Pride is also the engine behind egotism (thinking more of oneself than one ought) and behind false humility (putting oneself down to be less than what one actually is). Pride is the force behind resistance to lawful and appropriate authority — whether that authority is a parent, teacher, police officer, government, employer, or the Church.

Pride is the basis of thinking of oneself as better than others, being pompous, and having contempt toward one's neighbors, employers, other family members, or the Church and her ministers.

Pride can also rear its ugly head in more subtle ways such as reluctance to apologize when we need to apologize, demanding our rights merely because it is our right, being inappropriately unkind or rude, jealousy, being quick-tempered, moodiness, brooding over wrongs done by others to oneself, depression and despair, or demanding that we are right about something, when indeed we are right about the issue, even though the issue is unimportant or can be handled differently (this is a major phenomenon in marriages, families, and friendships — the phrase "We need to choose our battles" is an important remedy for this).

Other ways that Pride expresses itself include: by taking personal credit for gifts or possessions and thus refusing to acknowledge that we have what we have by God's Providence; glorying in our achievements as if they were not primary a result of God's grace and divine goodness; by minimizing one's defeats; by claiming qualities that are not actually possessed; magnifying the faults and defects of others or dwelling upon the defects and faults of others.

James 4:6-10 and 1 Peter 5:1-10 reveals that spiritual conflict follows pride.

Examine yourself for these and any other attributes of pride and then pray:

Dear Heavenly Father. You have said that pride goes before destruction and an arrogant spirit before stumbling (Prov. 16:18). I confess that I have not denied myself, picked up my cross daily, and followed You (Matt. 16:24). In so doing I have given ground to the enemy in my life. I have believed that I could be successful and live victoriously by my own strength and resources. I now confess that I have sinned against You by placing my will before You and by centering my life around self instead of You.

I now renounce the self-life and by so doing cancel all the ground that has been gained in my life by the enemies of the Lord Jesus Christ. I pray that You will guide me so that I will do nothing from selfishness or empty conceit, but with humility of mind that I will regard others as more important than myself (Phil. 2:3). Enable me through love to serve others and in honor prefer others (Rom. 12:10). Amen.

Rebellion: We often place our confidence in the flesh not only with the "I can do it myself" attitude but each time we assert our own opinions above the teachings of Christ. It is a pride and a rebellion to say, "I want to do it my way" or "I want to think the way I want" without regard to the ways God teaches us to go and to believe. This is an arrogance that not only can get us into major trouble but also forms a major vulnerability for demons to come into our life.

Rebelling against God and His authority gives Satan an opportunity to attack. As our commanding general, the Lord Jesus Christ says, *"Get into ranks and follow Me. I will not lead you into temptation, but I will deliver you from evil."*

The Bible teaches us that it is the will of God for us to be obedient to parents, to civil government, to the Church, and to the pastors who are over us. We have two biblical responsibilities in regard to these authority figures: 1) Pray for them; and 2) submit to them. The only time God permits us to disobey those in authority over us is when they require of us an act or acquiescence in ways that are contrary to Church Law, Natural Law, or Divine Law.

Being under authority is an act of faith; we are trusting God to work through His established lines of authority. The authority that God has ordained does not mean, however, that we are to submit to abuse from those authorities. In those cases where someone in authority over us is abusing us in any way, then we need to act in appropriate ways according to the situation — such as appeal to the state for protection and relief for civil or criminal issues; or appeal to Church authorities on some issue involving religion or our parish; or make appropriate decisions such as terminating an abusive relationship, etc. Whoever the authority, who is abusing, we need to pray for the offender and to forgive him; but we are not required to be a doormat or target of their abuse.

Some of the lines of authority mentioned in the Bible include:

- Church leaders (Hebrews 13:17; Matthew 18:15-18)
- Parents (Ephesians 6: 1-3; Exodus 20:12)
- Husbands (1 Peter 3:1-3; Ephesians 5:23-24)
- Employers (1 Peter 2:18-21)
- Civil Government (Romans 13:1-5; 1 Timothy 2:1-3; 1 Peter 2:13-16)

Examine yourself for any areas of rebellion (deliberate driving faster than the speed limit is rebellion, too, you know!) and then pray:

Dear Heavenly Father. You have said that rebellion is as the sin of witchcraft and insubordination is as iniquity and idolatry (1 Sam. 15.23). I know that in action and attitude I have sinned against You with a rebellious heart. I ask Your forgiveness for my rebellion and pray that by the shed blood of the Lord Jesus Christ, strengthened by intercession of the that all ground gained by evil spirits because of my rebelliousness be canceled and taken back. I pray that You will shed light on all my ways that I may know the full extent of my rebelliousness, and I now choose to adopt a submissive spirit and a servant's heart. Amen.

Unforgiveness: Jesus Himself discusses the seriousness of failing to forgive. He tells us that failure to forgive those who hurt us will result in our not being forgiven ourselves by God. *"Forgive us our trespasses (sins) as we forgive those who trespass (sin) against us"*. The *Our Father*, the Lord's Prayer, which most all of us know and pray, Jesus teaches us that God will be as forgiving to us as we are to others.

Indeed, how can we expect God to forgive us when we do not forgive our brothers? Consider the follow teachings from Holy Scripture:

If you forgive those who sin against you, your heavenly Father will forgive you. But if you refuse to forgive others, your Father will not forgive your sins (Matthew 6:14,15).

But when you are praying, first forgive anyone you are holding a grudge against, so that your Father in heaven will forgive your sins, too (Mark 11:25).

If you forgive others, you will be forgiven. (Luke 6:37b)

Forgiveness is not about emotions and feelings. You can still be hurting, angry and upset and still decide to forgive. Forgiveness involves a mental decision, a decision of will, an act of your free will, even though you may not "Feel it".

The true nature of forgiveness:

1. **Forgiveness is not forgetting:** People who try to forget find that cannot. It is an unfortunate quirk of the English language with the phrase, "Forgive and forget". In actuality this phrase does not mean to "forget" in the sense of not remembering what happened; of course, we will remember. God says He will "remember our sins no more" (Heb. 10: 17), but God, being omniscient, obviously cannot literally forget. "Remember no more" means that God will never use the past against us (Ps. 103:12).

   To forget is really "to let go". We need to *"let go and let God"*. We let go of the past, but more importantly we let go of the hurt. As long as we do not forgive, as long as we do not let go, we allow the offender of our wounds continue to hurt us.
2. **Forgiveness is a choice not a feeling:** Since God requires us to forgive, <u>it is something we can do</u>. God will NEVER ask us to do something that is impossible for us to do; that would be cruel and God is a loving God.

   Forgiveness, however, is difficult for us because it pulls against our feelings and emotional hurts. Forgiveness is not about forgetting our feelings or our emotional hurts. We often will not "feel" like forgiving, but we must forgive anyway. As the Lord Prayer teaches us, God forgives us "as we forgive others". But how can God require this of us when we have been hurt so badly?

   God does not expect your feelings and emotional hurts to be healed overnight. He knows and understands our feelings and our hurts. He is a compassionate God and will help us to heal over time, as we are able. What God expects of us is not an immediate emotional healing, but a decision of will to forgive, a decision of will to trust Him to take care of the offender and to heal us, a decision of will to ask God for, and to commit to, being healed of our wounds.

3. **Forgiveness is not letting the person off the hook:** Forgiving is about you letting go, but it is not letting the offender off the hook. He will still pay for what he did, either before the Law or before God or both.

   Forgiving is surely difficult for us because it pulls against our concept of justice. We want revenge for offenses suffered. But we are told never to take our own revenge (Rom. 12:9). Revenge does more damage to us than it punishes the offender. God's justice will prevail, no one can escape it. Never fear, those who hurt us will be held accountable, but we must let God deal with it. In order for God to deal with it, we need to let Him deal with it by letting go.

   "Why should I let them off the hook?" But doing that is precisely the problem — we are still hooked to them, still bound by our past when we do not forgive.

   To forgive does not mean letting the person off the hook; it means letting yourself off the hook.

4. **But you don't understand how much this person hurt me:** The problem is that when we do not forgive we, in essence, allow the person to still hurt us! The question is, "How do we stop the pain?" The answer is **to forgive!**

   It is important to understand that we do not forgive someone for their sake; we do it for our sake so we can be free. Our need to forgive is not an issue between the offender and us; it is between us and God.

5. **Forgiveness is agreeing to live with the consequences of another's sin:** Forgiveness is costly. We pay the price of the evil we forgive. We are going to live with those consequences whether we want to or not; our only choice is whether or not we will do so in the slavery of bitterness and unforgiveness or with the freedom of forgiveness.

   Jesus took the consequences of our sin upon Himself. All true forgiveness is substitution because no one really forgives without bearing the consequences of the other person's sin. God the Father *"made Him who knew no sin to be sin on our behalf, that we might become the righteousness of God in Him"* (2 Cor. 5:2 1).

   Where is the justice? We might ask. It is the Cross that makes forgiveness legally and morally right: *"For the death that He died, He died to sin, once for all"* (Rom. 6: 10). This doesn't mean that we tolerate sin. We must always stand against sin, but we must give the offender to God and get on with our life.

6. **How do we forgive from our heart?** First, we acknowledge the hurt and the hate. If our forgiveness does not visit the emotional core of our life, it will be incomplete. Many feel the pain of interpersonal offenses, but they will not

acknowledge it. Let God bring the pain to the surface so He can deal with it. This is where the healing takes place.

Do not wait to forgive until we feel like forgiving; we will never get there. Feelings take time to heal mostly _after_ the choice to forgive is made and Satan has lost his place (Eph. 4:26, 27). Freedom is what will be gained, not a feeling.

7. **Summary of Points on Forgiveness:**
   o Forgiveness is necessary to have fellowship with God.
   o It is not forgetting.
   o It is a choice.
   o Letting the offender off _our_ hook is what frees us.
   o The offender is not off God's hook.
   o God says, "Revenge is mine."
   o You must acknowledge the hurt and the hate.
   o Forgiveness means we are agreeing to live with the consequences of another's sin — which we have to do anyway.
   o The justice is in the cross.
   o Choice is between the slavery of bitterness or the freedom of forgiveness.
   o Forgiveness means not using the past against the offender.
   o Forgiveness _does not_ mean tolerating the sin or abuse.
   o Why forgive? To stop the pain! As we live in unforgiveness the offender still hurts us!
   o The issue of forgiveness is between you and God only.
   o The act of forgiveness is for your sake, and for your freedom.

Think about the people in your life for whom you need to forgive, people to whom you hold bitterness, people who have hurt you or disappointed you in anyway, or for whom you hold any kind of grudge. Be sure to ALWAYS include your parents, siblings, spouse, and YOURSELF. There is always something to forgive in our families and in ourselves.

Record all the names you can think of on a sheet of paper and a brief note as to why you need to forgive them. If you do not remember names, list them by what you do remember, such as "the guy in sixth grade with the red hat". If you cannot remember why you need to forgive someone on your list that is okay; forgive them for whatever it was — God knows.

After preparing this list ask God to bring to your mind anyone you have forgotten. It is not unusual to forget, or to push aside from our conscious mind, incidents and even the names of people whom have hurt us. These hidden hurts and wounds need to be healed as well. Thus, ask God to bring to your mind any person you have forgotten for whom you need to forgive, for whom you hold a grudge against, for which you are bitter, for those who have hurt you, with the following prayer:

Father in heaven, please bring to my mind the names of any people for whom I have held bitterness towards, grudges against, or have not forgiven for the hurts they have caused me. Help me to remember all these hurts so that they may be offered to You, O Lord, and healed from my soul so that I may live the truly victorious Christ-life. Amen.

Add to your list the names of anyone God may bring to your mind.

Now it is time to pray...

The following prayer needs to be said for each person on the list for which you need to forgive. Do not go to the next person on the list until you are sure you have dealt with all the remembered pain.

As you pray, God may bring to your mind various offending people and experiences that has been totally forgotten. Allow God to do this even if it is painful. Remember this process of forgiveness is for your sake because God wants you to be free.

Remember also that by forgiving the offender we are not rationalizing or trying to explain the offender's behavior. Forgiveness deals with the victim's pain, your pain, not another's excuses. Positive feelings will follow in time; freeing you from the past is the critical issue now.

If you are willing to forgive for your sake, so that you can walk away from this webpage free in Christ, free from the past and from person who hurt you, pray the introductory prayer below and then pray the "Prayer to Forgive" for each person on your list:

Heavenly Father, I now ask for your help in forgiving all those people on my list. Although I am still hurt and angry with them, I know that they are your children and that you love them more than I can possibly know. For this reason, my God, I ask you to help me forgive them. I lay down all bitterness, resentment and hatred for this person and I freely choose to forgive them. Teach me to be more merciful, my God, and help me be always willing, just as you are always willing, to forgive those who sin against me. Amen."

Prayer to Forgive

Lord, I forgive _______________________________ for (specifically identify all offenses and painful memories).

May God heal you and bless you!

Step 5 — Know Who You Are in Christ!

In order to gain freedom, it is important to know who you are in Christ. Thus, you need to evaluate the concept you have of yourself, to acknowledge the truth about God and about yourself; about your relationship and ideas about God and about the manner of our lives.

We often deceive ourselves about our position in Christ and our relationship with Him. For example, we may say to ourselves: "This isn't going to work" or "I wish I could believe this but I can't" or perhaps even more direct deceptions or denials concerning the promises of God for His children. Areas of deception that we may have include:

1. **Self-Deception** (telling ourselves things that are not true)

- o Listening to God's words but thinking we do not have to do it (Ja 1:22; 4:17)
- o Thinking we have no sin or do not sin (1 Jn 1:8)
- o Thinking that we are something when we are not (Gal 6:3)
- o Believing that we will not reap what we sow (Gal 6:7)
- o Thinking we are wise and sophisticated in the 21st century (1 Cor 3:18, 19)
- o Believing that the unrighteous will reach heaven (1 Cor 6:9)
- o Thinking we can associate with bad company and not be corrupted (1 Cor 15:33)

2. **Self-Defense** (defending ourselves instead of trusting Christ)
- o Denial (conscious or subconscious)
- o Fantasy (escape from the real world)
- o Emotional insulation (withdraw to avoid rejection)
- o Regression (reverting back to a less threatening time in the past)
- o Displacement (taking out frustrations on others)
- o Projection (blaming others or accusing others of things we ourselves have done)
- o Rationalization (defending self though verbal excursion)

To counter these and other deceptions we tell ourselves we need to exercise faith. Faith is the response to Truth and believing the truth is a CHOICE (not a feeling). If we say, "I want to believe God, but I just can't," then we are deceiving ourselves. Of course, we can believe God. We know that God does not lie. Faith is something we DECIDE to do; it is not something we FEEL like doing. Believing the truth does not make it true; rather it is TRUE, therefore we believe it.

Examine yourself and how you may deceive yourself with "self-deceptions" and "Self-Defense" mechanisms. The pray the following prayer: ...

Prayer to Know the Truth:

Dear Heavenly Father. I know that You desire truth in the inner self and that facing this truth is the way of liberation (John 8:32). I acknowledge that I have been deceived by the father of lies (John 8:44) and that I have deceived myself (1 John 1:8). I pray in the name of the Lord Jesus Christ, and since by faith I have received You into my life and am now seated with Christ in the heavenliest (Eph 2:6), I ask you Father to command all deceiving spirits to depart from me. I now ask You to *"search me, O God, and know my heart: try me and know my anxious thoughts; and see if there be any hurtful way in me, and lead me in the everlasting way"* (Ps. 139:23, 24) In the name of Christ Jesus I pray. Amen.

Knowing the truth about oneself, overcoming self-deceptions and the mechanism of self-defense that hide who we really are, includes understanding our faith in Christ. It is by Christ that our lives have meaning and substance.

The following prayer is the substance of that faith:

Affirmations

I believe that I am a child of God (1 Jn. 3:1-3) and that I am seated with Christ in the heavenlies (Eph. 2:6). I believe that I was saved by the grace of God through faith that is a gift and not the result of my own efforts or merits (Eph 2:8).

I choose to be strong in the Lord and in the strength of His might (Eph 6:10). I put no confidence in the flesh (Phil 3:3) for the weapons of warfare are not of the flesh (2 Cor. 10:4). I put on the whole armor of God (Eph. 6:10-20), and I resolve to stand firm in my faith and to resist the evil one.

I believe that Jesus Christ has all authority in heaven and on earth (Matt 28:18) and that He is the head over all rule and authority (Col 2:10). I believe that Satan and his demons and wicked spirits are subject to the Lord Jesus Christ and therefore to me in Christ since I am a member of Christ's body (Eph 1:19-23).

I believe that apart from Christ I can do nothing (John 15:5) so I declare my dependence upon Him.

I choose to abide in Christ in order to bear much fruit and to glorify the Lord (Jn 15:8) and to accomplish the work of sanctification that Christ began in me through the Cross (James 2).

I believe that since I am a member go God's royal family I have the authority, in the name of Christ Jesus, to ask the Father to command the devil to leave my presence, as I obey the command to resist the devil (James 4:7).

I reject any counterfeit gifts or works of Satan and his minions in my life.

I believe that the truth will set me free (John 8:32) and that walking in the light is the only path of fellowship and freedom (1 John 1:7). Therefore, as a royal member of God's household, I stand against Satan's deceptions by affirming all the doctrines of the Faith and by taking every thought captive in obedience to Christ (2 Cor 10:5).

I declare that the Bible and the Church are the only authoritative standards for me (2 Tim 3:15, 16).

I choose to speak the truth in love (Eph 4:15).

I choose to present my body as an instrument of righteousness, a living and holy sacrifice, and thus I renew my mind daily by the living Word of God in order that I may prove that the will of God is good, acceptable, and perfect (Rom 6:13; 12:1, 2).

I ask my heavenly Father to fill me with His Holy Spirit (Eph 5:18), to lead me into all truth (John 16:13), and to empower my life that I may live above sin and not carry out the desires of the flesh (Gal 5:16). I crucify the flesh (Gal 5:24) and choose to walk by the Spirit.

In making all these affirmations, I renounce all selfish goals and choose the ultimate goal of love (1 Tim 1:5). I choose to obey the greatest commandment to love the Lord my God will all my heart, soul, and mind, and to love my neighbor as myself (Matt 22:37-39). Amen.

Step 6 — Worship, Pray, and Fast

Worship as a Church Family: One of Satan's favorite lies, apart from having us believe that he does not exist, or that he does exist and is more powerful than he truly is, is that since God is everywhere and we can worship Him anywhere and do not need the "community of believers ", the Church family.

Although it is true that God is everywhere and worshiping Him anywhere is wholesome and good, it is false to believe that the Church is unnecessary. Since the earliest days of Christianity, communities of believers gathered together on the *Lord's Day* (Sunday).

Scripture is very clear on the subject of Church attendance and on how our submission to its authority is not only good but required. The Church, its leaders and members, are the Mystical Body of Christ here on Earth. To disobey the teachings of the Church as it relates to faith and morals is to disobey the teachings of Christ. To not attend church is also disobedience to Christ.

Paul admonishes those who do not come to Church in Hebrews 10:19-25:

Therefore, brothers, since through the blood of Jesus we have confidence of entrance into the sanctuary by the new and living way he opened for us through the veil, that is, his flesh, and since we have "a great priest over the house of God," let us approach with a sincere heart and in absolute trust, with our hearts sprinkled clean from an evil conscience and our bodies washed in pure water. Let us hold unwaveringly to our confession that gives us hope, for he who made the promise is trustworthy. We must consider how to rouse one another to love and good works. We should not stay away from our assembly, as is the custom of some, but encourage one another, and this all the more as you see the day drawing near.

Hebrews 13:17

Obey your leaders and submit to them; for they are keeping watch over your souls, as men who will have to give account. Let them do this joyfully, and not sadly, for that would be of no advantage to you.

Worship and prayer together as a family, prayer meetings, adoration, and other corporate settings, and in the privacy of the family at home is critical in developing spiritual health for the family and each family member. Such family devotion forms the foundation for all that each family does away from home in the world of school, work, and society.

Prayer is so important both in the family context and individually. It is important not just because prayer is something a Christian ought to do, but because prayer is communication.

The more we depend on God, the closer He is to us and we are to Him. Aligning ourselves with God, communicating with Him at all times and in all situations and personal decisions will unite our hearts to His. A heart united to the Creator will overflow with graces and blessings.

Prayer and Spiritual Warfare: In addition, a healthy prayer life destroys strongholds that demons may have in our lives and in our hearts. Without prayer we cannot hope to be delivered from spiritual afflictions. It is no secret —prayer, worship, devotion, and living the Christ-Life in all that it entails is the formula not only for deliverance from spiritual afflictions, but for living the victorious life in Christ.

When dealing with spiritual afflictions, however, some special prayer considerations may be needed. Scripture states that there are certain demons that will only respond to prayer as well as fasting: *"But this kind does not go out except by prayer and fasting."* (Matthew 17:21). If fasting can defeat even the strongest of fallen angels, just how powerful is this sacrifice that we can make?

Spiritual warfare prayers are very effective in defeating the enemy and drawing our hearts closer to God.

Step 7 — Live the Faith and Remain Faithful

Along with all the advice and recommendations of the first six steps, our healing and deliverance cannot be complete unless we act upon our faith. Doing good works and charitable acts of love are a natural outflow of our faith and necessary to lead a good Christian life. It is not enough to believe. James asks and admonishes in James 2:19,20, 26:

Do you still think it's enough just to believe that there is one God? Well, even the demons believe this, and they tremble in terror! Fool! When will you ever learn that faith that does not result in good deeds is useless?

Just as the body is dead without a spirit, so also faith is dead without good deeds.

James calls a man a fool who does not act upon his faith in James 1:22-25:

Be doers of the word and not hearers only, deluding yourselves. For if anyone is a hearer of the Word and not a doer, he is like a man who looks at his own face in a mirror. He sees himself, then goes off and promptly forgets what he looks like. But the one who peers into the prefect law of freedom and perseveres, and is not a hearer who forgets but a doer who acts, such a one shall be blessed in what he does.

It is hard to live the Christ-Life, but we must try. We must not have a faith that is dead and useless. We must not be a fool and not practice our faith. We must, rather, live out our faith and persevere in the faith:

1 Corinthians 9:23-27

All this I do for the sake of the gospel, so that I too may have a share in it. Do you not know that the runners in the stadium all run in the race, but only one wins the prize? Run so as to win. Every athlete exercises discipline in every way. They do it to win a perishable crown, but we an imperishable one. Thus, I do not run aimlessly; I do not fight as if I were shadowboxing. No, I drive my body and train it, for fear that, after having preached to others, I myself should be disqualified.

Colossians 1:17-23

He is before all things, and in him all things hold together. He is the head of the body, the church. He is the beginning, the firstborn from the dead, that in all things he himself might be preeminent. For in him all the fullness was pleased to dwell, and through him to reconcile all things for him, making peace by the blood of his cross (through him), whether those on earth or those in heaven.

And you who once were alienated and hostile in mind because of evil deeds he has now reconciled in his fleshly body through his death, to present you holy, without blemish, and irreproachable before him, provided that you persevere in the faith, firmly grounded, stable, and not shifting from the hope of the gospel that you heard, which has been preached to every creature under heaven, of which I, Paul, am a minister.

And thus, let us be able to say, with St. Paul, in 2 Timothy 4:6-8

For I am already on the point of being sacrificed; the time of my departure has come. I have fought the good fight, I have finished the race, I have kept the faith. Henceforth there is laid up for me the crown of righteousness, which the Lord, the righteous judge, will award to me on that Day, and not only to me but also to all who have loved His appearing.

Persevere in the faith and let your life be a living Gospel for you shall thereby *know the truth and the truth shall set you free*

I have outlined steps detailing certain issues that we have found important in gaining freedom for a person in spiritual affliction.

1. purify one's conscience by a good confession;
2. Receive Holy Communion as often as possible;
3. Implore the mercy of God by prayer and fasting.
4. Recourse to specific spiritual warfare prayers applicable to the situation.

Final Thoughts

Repentance, forgiveness, acting on our faith, praying, fasting, receiving the Sacrament frequently, and all the rest we ought to do as good Christians are very good things and very necessary for this life, but more importantly for the life to come.

The advice contained in these Steps to Self-Deliverance, however, are not "quick fixes". This advice involves a lifelong commitment for anyone with spiritual afflictions. Freeing yourself from the bondages of the enemy and keeping them from returning requires this commitment to persevere in Christ and in the Christ-life.

There will be dry times. Your faith will be tested. Indeed, the demons may (and more than likely will) try to return. Scripture speaks of what demons do once they are cast out:

Now when the unclean spirit goes out of a man, it passes through waterless places seeking rest, and does not find it. Then it says, 'I will return to my house from which I came'; and when it comes, it finds it unoccupied, swept, and put in order. Then it goes and takes along with it seven other spirits more wicked than itself, and they go in and live there; and the last state of that man becomes worse than the first. (Matthew 12, 43-45).

Do not leave your house (heart) *"unoccupied, swept and put in order"*; rather be filled with the Holy Spirit.

We can never let down our guard. As a final instruction, remember the teaching of St. Paul in Ephesians 6:10-18. We do not go about our day without putting on our clothes. Do not go into the world with God's armor:

Finally, draw your strength from the Lord and from his mighty power. Put on the armor of God so that you may be able to stand firm against the tactics of the devil. For our struggle is not with flesh and blood but with the principalities, with the powers, with the world rulers of this present darkness, with the evil spirits in the heavens. Therefore, put on the armor of God that you may be able to resist on the evil day and, having done everything, to hold your ground. So, stand fast with your loins girded in truth, clothed with righteousness as a breastplate, and your feet shod in readiness for the gospel of peace. In all circumstances, hold faith as a shield, to quench all (the) flaming arrows of the evil one. And take the helmet of salvation and the sword of the Spirit, which is the word of God. With all prayer and supplication, pray at every opportunity in the Spirit. To that end, be watchful with all perseverance and supplication.

APENDEX 1
Steps for Self-Deliverance

The purpose of all this information is to enable you to do a self-deliverance at home for yourself. The process of self-deliverance is carried out in stages. Let's go through them one by one.

STEP ONE: Start with praise and worship. You can sing songs to praise God and to worship Him.

STEP TWO: Confess out loud Scriptures promising deliverance. Luke 10:19, Ephesians 1:7, Romans 16:20, Revelation 12:11, Colossians 2:14-15, Galatians 3:13-14, Psalms 91:3…_2 Timothy 4:18_ says And the Lord shall deliver me from every evil work, and will preserve me unto His heavenly kingdom: to whom be glory forever and ever. Amen. You should memorize _2 Tim 4:18_.

STEP THREE: Break covenants and curses to destroy their legal hold. You pray a simple prayer like this: I break any curse or covenant working against me, in the name of Jesus. (Simple prayers)

STEP FOUR: Bind all the spirits associated with those covenants and curses like this: I bind all the spirits attached or connected to the curses and covenants I have just broken, in the name of Jesus.

STEP FIVE: Lay one hand on your head and pray, Holy Ghost, cover me from the top of my head to the sole of my feet, in the name of Jesus. Begin to mention every organ of your body; kidney, liver, intestine, blood, etc. You must not rush at this level. Lay your hands-on areas that the Spirit of God leads you to.

STEP SIX: Then begin to saturate yourself with the Blood of Jesus. You do this by saying: I plead the Blood of Jesus over me. This must continue until you have a release in your spirit to stop.

STEP SEVEN: It is now, that you can demand firmly, in the name of the Lord Jesus Christ, that any spirit that is not of God should leave you. You demand it forcefully like this: In the name of the Lord Jesus Christ, I come against all you hidden spirits and I bind your activities in my life. You can no longer hide below the surface because I now recognize what you have been doing; release me, in the name of Jesus.

(If sickness is the problem, address it and say) You spirit of infirmity, I speak to you directly, get out of my life now. I am redeemed by the Blood of Jesus Christ, come out and go now. Go out with every breath by the power of the Holy Spirit. I prevail over you, in the name of Jesus.

STEP EIGHT: Ask for a fresh in-filling of the Holy Spirit and close the session with praises. Self-deliverance keeps you from getting sick; it removes every evil seed of the enemy; it charges your body with fire. It uproots evil plantations and builds up your confidence. Every night before you go to bed, you must remember these two important prayer points.

1. Pray for cover with the Blood of Jesus. **_Revelation 12:11_** = And they overcame him by the Blood of the Lamb, and by the word of their testimony; and they loved not their lives unto the death.
2. Pray that the Angels of God should surround you. **_Psalms 34:7_** = The Angel of the Lord encampeth round about them that fear him, and delivereth them.

No matter how sleepy you are, make sure pray these two prayer points every night. There is no reason why self-deliverance should not be effective. However, if the person seeking deliverance is under stubborn demonic control or hereditary strongman and lacks sufficient faith or authority to defeat the oppressors or living in any known sin, the evil spirits will be hard to get rid of. right.

One final word of caution. For a person to be delivered, he/she must want deliverance. Self-deliverance must not be done because of pride, shyness, the fear of possible public embarrassment, etc. Your motive for engaging in self-deliverance has to be pure.

REMEMBER: **_DELIVERANCE IS A PROCESS (((NOT A ONE-TIME EVENT)))_** AND THE LENGTH OF TIME IT TAKES DEPENDS ON SEVERAL THINGS;

1. The length of time the spirit has stayed inside a person
2. The strength and reinforcement of the spirit
3. The experience and degree of anointing upon those who are ministering the deliverance
4. The willingness of the person being delivered to be free
5. The knowledge of the Word of God and your level of hatred for sin
6. SELF-DISCIPLINE IS NECESSARY

Also, remember that bondage can be weak or strong. A weak hold can be broken quickly, whereas a stronghold may take a more time. You will not realize the strength of bondage until you faithfully and persistently work on it. You must remember that a foothold can graduate to a stronghold if left unaddressed. After this exercise, set aside some days (with fasting). DO NOT CONTINUE TO DO THE THINGS THAT CAUSED THE "it"! CHANGE YOUR HABITS TO AGREE WITH YOUR PRAYERS. AMEN.

Appendix 2

Exposing the Doors to Bondage

Part I: The bondage

1. When did this bondage start?

2. Was there any unusual things that took place (or you did) when this bondage started?

3. If this bondage started when you were a child: Do you have ancestors who have suffered from a similar kind of bondage?

4. What kind of bondage are you facing? (Fears, depression, voices in your mind, mental illness, physical illness, mental torment, spiritual torment, etc... Please be as detailed as possible.)

5. What are all the things that have impacted your life? (Parent's death, trauma, a certain situation that changed your life, anything that 'changed' you.)

Part II: Your ancestor's background

1. Do you have ancestors who have struggled with similar problems or bondages?

2. Did your bondage start as a child and appear to have no reason to be there?

3. Do you have siblings who suffer from similar bondages or oppression?

Part III: Soul ties

1. Have you been involved with extramarital sex? Are you attracted to an ex-lover? Is he or she a good/godly influence for you?

2. Have you been divorced?

3. Do you feel an unusual attraction to a past boyfriend, girlfriend or lover (who is obviously not right for you)?

4. Do you let anybody dominate, control, or make your choices you?

5. Have you ever formed a blood covenant with another person? (Blood brothers, etc.)

6. Have you ever made vows or agreements with somebody in effort to strengthen the relationship or commit yourself to each other?

7. Do you see any ungodly relationships in your past where gifts were exchanged? (Are you holding onto something that was given to you from somebody you had adultery with, etc.)

8. Have you ever had ungodly relations with any one?

9. Do you have any pictures in your possession of somebody whom you may have an ungodly soul tie with? (A picture of you with somebody you had an adultery with, etc.)

Part IV: Relationship with parents

1. What do you think of your parents?

2. How would you explain your childhood?

3. Where you close to your parents while growing up? If not, why?

4. How would you explain your relationship with your parents? Was it good, bad or very cold?

5. Did you feel rejection from your parents?

6. Was either of your parents overly passive or controlling?

7. Has either of your parents been divorced? Remarried? Are your parents divorced?

8. How would you describe your relationship with your siblings growing up?

Part V: Rejection and abuse

1. Were your parents married when you were conceived? Were you the right sex? Did your parents not want you, or want you to be different (gender, etc.) in any way? If so, explain.

2. Did you feel rejected as a child? As an adult? If so, by whom? Explain.

3. Did you face abuse? What kind (emotional, physical, sexual, etc.) and by whom?

4. Have you faced rejection from your peers, classmates, friends or those around you?

5. Have you ever been put down, belittled, or made fun of? If so, by whom? Explain.

6. If you have faced rejection or abuse, how did you respond? Do you feel you are still paying a price for it? If so, how?

7. How do you respond to rejection right now?

8. Do you reject yourself (self-rejection)? If so, why and in what ways?

Part VI: Unforgiveness or bitterness

1. Is there anybody you feel edgy around? (Don't like them, feel anything in your heart against them, etc.)

2. Do you have anything against anybody? In other words, is there anybody that you have a hard time demonstrating the love of Christ to?

3. Has anybody wronged you that you haven't forgiven from your heart (thoughts, feelings, emotions, etc.)?

4. How do your view your siblings, parents, coworkers, etc.? Do you have any hard feelings against them?

5. Do you make a habit of blaming yourself for everything? Do you obsess over your mistakes and feel unusually guilty for them?

6. Do you deeply regret things that you've done in your past? Could you kick yourself over something you've done in your past? If so, explain.

Part VII: Personality

1. Are you a very positive or negative person?

2. Do you feel confident in yourself? If so, why?

3. Do you have a low self-esteem? If so, why?

4. Are you domineering or controlling? If so, to whom, and in what ways? Why?

5. Are you an achiever? (A go-getter) If so, in what ways?

6. Do you feel that you are always right and that if everybody did everything your way, this world would be a better place to live?

7. How do you treat your children? Husband? Are you controlling, passive, etc.?

8. Do you like people to 'look at you' (as in receive attention)?

Part VIII: Emotional health

1. Do you strive to feel accepted? If so, how does this affect your lifestyle? By whom do you want to feel accepted?

2. Are you always stressed out? If so, why?

3. Do you feel hurt? If so, by whom/what and why?

4. Do you feel good about yourself? If not, why?

5. Do you feel depressed? If so, why? When did it start? Did your parents or grandparents struggle with depression? If so, then do you know when it started and why? Do you have siblings who are also struggling? Do you feel your depression is rational or irrational?

6. Do you struggle with fears? If so, what is it that you fear? (Fear of heights, dying, being hopeless, failure, never marrying, etc.)

7. Do you worry about things? What things do you worry about? Why?

8. Do you struggle with anger? Do you have a short temper?

9. Do you have any insecurity? If so, explain.

10. Do you feel any self-pity or feel sorry for yourself? Have you ever felt this? If so, why?

11. Do you find it easy to hate people? If so, over what kinds of things would a person have to do to make you hate them?

12. Do you have any irrational feelings? If so, what are they?

13. Do you feel like something is wrong with you?

14. Do you feel excessively guilty over anything? Is this a continual problem?

15. Are you very confused and forgetful? (Beyond the normal)

16. Are you aware of any emotional wounds that have affected you?

17. Have you ever been deeply embarrassed over something? What was it?

18. Have you been in or are currently experiencing very difficult (depressing) circumstances which may cause you to feel hopeless or depressed?

Part IX: Who are you in Christ? And how do you see God?

1. How do you explain your relationship with God?

2. Do you feel you aren't good enough to meet His standards?

3. Do you see Him as a loving father, or a dictator?

4. Do you believe that it's only by the Blood of Jesus that your sins are forgiven? Or do you feel you need to earn your forgiveness in any way?

5. Do you feel God's love in your life?

6. Do you feel like your sins are forgiven? Or do you feel guilty?

7. Do you feel excessively guilty in everyday life?

8. Do you feel that doing good things, you earn God's love and acceptance?

9. Do you feel that God is angry or upset with you?

Part X: Spoken curses, vows & oaths

1. Have you ever spoken something negative about yourself that has come to past? For example: "I'm sick and tired..." or "If I don't quit typing, I'm going to get arthritis!"

2. Has your parents, or those in authority over you spoken out a curse over you? For example: "You'll never amount to anything!" or "You'll never get out of debt" or "You're so dumb"

3. Have you ever made a vow out of anger? If so, what? For example: "I'll never let anybody push me around again!" or "I'm never going to be hurt again!"

4. Have you ever wished to die? Have you ever said it?

5. If you have made any vows or oaths, what are they?

Part XI: Relationships

1. Do you have many friends? What kind of people are they?

2. Do you have a hard time trying to meet new people or make friends?

3. Are you socially outgoing or shy? If so, why?

4. How would you define your relationship with your spouse?

Part XII: Sexuality

1. Have you ever had unholy sex? What kind? (Fornication, adultery, sodomy, with a child, etc.)

2. Have you struggled with lust, fantasy or unholy sexual thoughts? If so, what kind?

3. Have you been attracted to pornography?

4. Do you have homosexual thoughts and desires? If so, have you acted upon those feelings?

5. How do you feel about your sexuality? (Do you feel dirty about it, or do you feel it's a wonderful blessing that God's given you?)

6. Do you withhold sex from your spouse or are you fidgety? Do you enjoy a healthy relationship with your spouse sexually? How does he or she react?

7. Have you ever been raped or sexually abused?

8. Have you ever woke up and felt a sexual presence with you? There are demons that imitate male and female functions, and stimulate their host (a person) sexually (beyond the normal 'wet dream').

9. Do you struggle or have you struggled with masturbation?

10. Do you struggle or have you struggled with any other sexual related thoughts, desires, or bondages?

11. Is there anything sexually that you are ashamed of?

Part XIII: Addictions

1. Do you have any addictions? If so, what kind? (Drugs, alcohol, smoking, eating, sex, TV, etc.) When did they start?

2. Did anybody else in your family (siblings, ancestors, etc.) have a struggle with any addictions? If so, what? Who?

3. Have you ever had, or currently have any sort of obsession over anything? If so, what?

Part XIV: False religions

Examples of false religions: Buddhism, Hindu, Jehovah Witness, Mormonism, Christian Scientists, eastern religions, etc.

1. Have you ever been involved with any false religions? If so, why, when and how long? How do you feel about those beliefs now?

2. Have you ever been involved in any secret societies such as Freemasonry? If so, how deep were you involved?

Part XV: The occult

1. Have you ever shown interest in the occult? If so, in what ways? (Read up on it, dabbled in it, etc.)

2. Do you still feel drawn or attracted to the occult?

3. Have you had any interest in horror or thriller style movies or novels? Are you still attracted to these things?

4. Have you ever made a vow with the devil? If so, what?

5. Married Satan?

6. Worshipped a demon or Satan?

7. Have you ever put a curse or spell on somebody?

8. Are you aware of any curses or spells placed on you? If so, what? Who did it?

9. Dabbled with an Ouija board? If so, why?

10. Ever been a member of a coven (group of 13 witches)? Explain.

11. Communicated with the dead? Explain.

12. Told somebody's fortune or went to see a fortune teller? Explain.

13. Ever read your horoscope?

14. Watched or been involved in a séance? Explain.

15. Have you been involved or a victim of Satanic Ritual Abuse (SRA)? Explain.

16. Been baptized into a false religion or any other evil baptism? If so, what were you baptized into? When?

17. Have you ever had a spirit guide?

18. Have you ever been involved with meditation, yoga, karate, or related activities?

19. Were you or anybody in your family superstitious? If so, who?

20. Ever been involved in astral travel? (Out of body)

21. If you have made any vows or oaths, what are they? Were there any sacrifices or rituals that were accompanied with them?

22. Have you ever made a blood pact before? If so, with whom (including persons, demons and Satan) and for what purpose?

23. Have you ever partaken in automatic writing, automatic drawing or automatic painting?

24. Have you ever been involved in Yoga, transcendental meditation, or similar activities?

25. Have you ever sought healing from a spiritual source other than Jesus Christ? (New age healing, energy healing, etc.)

26. Any other involvement in the occult? Explain.

Part XVI: Un-confessed sins

1. Are there any un-confessed sins that you have not repented of? (Usually something you've done, that you know is wrong, but won't admit to it. An abortion, stealing, etc. are some examples.)

2. Is there anything you've been hiding inside that you haven't confessed?

3. Do you feel excessively guilty over something(s) you've done in the past? If so, what?

Part XVII: Cursed objects

1. Do you have any idols, occult rings, or anything that could hold evil spiritual value in your home? If so, what? Any objects that hold evil spiritual value must be destroyed.

2. Do you have any gifts saved from sinful relationships? If so, explain. For example, if a man gives a woman a personal gift during an adultery that needs to be sold or destroyed.

Part XVIII: Severe trauma, abuse & disassociation

1. Have you ever been exposed to extreme abuse or a traumatic experience? Did it have a drastic effect on your emotional or mental system? If so, what happen? How did it affect you?

2. Have you ever disassociated or been diagnosed with Dissociative Identity Disorder (DID) or Multiple Personality Disorder (MPD)?

3. Are you aware of any alters (other personalities) that you may have? (If so, tell me about them)

4. Do you have a memory gap where you cannot remember a certain time of your life?

5. Do you have false memories of things that really didn't take place?

6. Have you ever been in a car accident or other traumatic situation? Have you ever witnessed a tragedy in real life?

Part XIX: Weaknesses

1. Do you struggle with any habitual sins? If so, what? Do you want to break those bad habits?

2. Do you struggle with any weaknesses such as lust, anger, hate, etc.? If so, what? Do you know where they came from or how they got started? Do you want to break free from those weaknesses?

Part XX: Pregnancy issues

1. Have you ever said something along the lines of, "I will never have children"?

2. Have you ever had an abortion or attempted one?

3. Have you ever had incest or ungodly sexual relations with somebody related to you? (See Leviticus 20:19-21, as this can cause a curse to land upon you which needs to be broken)

Part XXI: Other things to look for

1. Have you ever tried drugs? If so, how much, and how did it affect you? Why did you try drugs?

2. Have you ever thought about or attempted suicide?

3. Do you have any physical or mental disabilities, diseases or illnesses? Explain.

4. Do you want, and are willing to be delivered? Are you willing to give up those demon spirits and maybe make some lifestyle changes in order to keep your deliverance?

5. Do you experience unusual confusion settle upon you as you try to pray and read the Bible?

6. What kind of music do you like? (Please list all styles of music you currently enjoy, and give examples in each category you list, such as some names of artists and songs)

7. Have you previously enjoyed hard rock, metal, acid, alternative, rap, new age, or any other kind of worldly music? (Please provide some examples of artists and songs from each genre (type/style) of music you list)

8. Have you had any nightmares or weird experiences at night while supposedly sleeping?

9. Have you ever been in a trance or had an out of body experience?

10. Have you ever noticed time slipped right out from under you? For example, you look at your watch and its 7:00pm, then you look again what seemed like 15 minutes later and its 2:00am. This is a sign of a trance.

11. Have you ever touched or kissed a dead body? If so, explain whom and why and what happened afterwards.

12. Do you feel that you somehow have to earn your forgiveness? Do you 'wonder' if your sins are truly forgiven -- all of them? Are you aware of any signs of legalism or religious spirits operating in your mind?

13. Do you have any physical infirmities, sickness or diseases? If so, please list them.

14. Are you on any medications? If so, please explain.

15. Are you entertained by movies or TV shows which glorify death, murder, pain or suffering of others? Please explain.

16. Have you ever had any other kind of weird encounter with the spiritual realm?

Use this information to expose the root cause of the "it".

REFERENCES

1. Gary R. Collins, *Christian Counseling: A Comprehensive Guide*, 3rd Addition, Revised and Updated, NavPress, Colorado Springs, Colorado. ISBN 1418503290
2. Beilby, J.K. & P.R. Eddy. *Understanding Spiritual Warfare: Four Views*. Grand Rapids, Michigan: Baker, 2012.
3. Boyd, G.A., *God at War: The Bible and Spiritual Conflict*. Downers Grove, Illinois: IVP, 1997.
4. Hiebert, P. "Spiritual Warfare and Worldview"
5. Stedman, R.C, *Spiritual Warfare: Winning the Daily Battle with Satan*. Portland, Oregon: Multnomah, 1975.
6. Pirolo, N., *Prepare for Battle: Basic Training in Spiritual Warfare*, San Diego, California: Emmaus Road, International, 1997.
7. Arnold, E. C., *3 Crucial Questions about Spiritual Warfare*, Grand Rapids, Michigan: Baker, 1997.l
8. Rita Bennett, You Can Be Emotionally Free, 1982 ISBN 978 0 88270 748 8
9. Rita Bennett, Emotionally Free, 1982, ISBN 0 86065 194 0 Publishers, PO Box 777,
10. Tonbridge, Kent TN 11 0ZS, England, 1997, reprinted 2004). ISBN 1-85240-110-9. (Available in the US through the Arsenal Bookstore, 11005 Voyager Parkway, Colorado Springs, CO 80921.)
11. John and Paula Sandford, Healing the Wounded Spirit (Victory House, 1985). ISBN 0-932081-14-2.
12. Norma Dearing, The Healing Touch (Chosen Books, 2002). ISBN 0-8007-9302-1. Charles Kraft, Deep Wounds, Deep Healing (Servant Pub., 1993). ISBN 0-89283-784-5.
13. Derek Prince, God's Remedy for Rejection (Whitaker House, 1993). ISBN 088368-864-6.
14. Francis and Judith MacNutt, Praying for Your Unborn Child (1989). ISBN 0-38523-2829. (Available from www.Christianhealingmin.org, 904-765-3332.)
15. Thomas Verney, MD, The Secret Life of the Unborn Child (Summit Books, 1981).
16. Anderson, Winning Spiritual Warfare 1990 ISBN 13: 978-0-89081-868-8 James
17. Friesen, Uncovering the Mystery of MPD, 1997 ISBN 1-56819-062-7
18. Diane Hawkins, Multiple Identities, 2009 ISBN 978-0-9708073-6-6,
19. Restoration in Christ Ministries, http://www.rcm-usa.org/index.htm
20. Francis MacNutt, Deliverance from Evil Spirits, 1995, 0-8007-9232-7, Chap 17, pp 223-235 (best introductory material)
21. Daniel Ryder, Breaking the Circle of SRA, 1992, 0-89638-258-3 (an excellent book by a Christian counselor)
22. Margaret Smith, Ritual Abuse, what it is, why it happens, how to help, 1993, 0-06-250214-X (in depth information about SRA and MPD)
23. The Christian Bible
24. The following associations focus on trauma and disassociation www.sidran.org, www.issd.org
25. Pentecost, J.D., *Your Adversary the Devil*. Grand Rapids, Michigan: Zondervan, 1969

About the Author
Dr. Paulette Douglas

Dr. Paulette Douglas truly epitomizes elegance in living a saved, sanctified and Holy life, set apart from the secular world! Dr. Douglas is an ordained minister with the Pentecostal Assemblies of the World, an anointed national and international Evangelist, teacher and preacher. Dr. Paulette Douglas is renowned for the ministry of exhortation to the Body of Christ through deliverance, inner healing, salvation and biblical counseling at seminars, prayer clinics, crusades and conferences. She has established three churches and assisted in establishing many other churches, ministries and colleges as she serves on the Body of Christ for Jesus. Dr. Douglas was baptized in the name of Jesus Christ and filled with the Holy Ghost in 1977. She was called to the ministry in 1981, taught bible study at Pacific Bell for nine years which established the Radiant Life in Christ Ministries. She was the founder and pastor of the Radiant Life in Christ Community Church in Baldwin Park, California for nearly four years. Dr. Douglas retired in 1996 with full benefits from AT&T after 26 years of service. God introduced Dr. Douglas to the LOVE and HERO of her life, Bishop Robert T. Douglas Sr. They were married, the ministries merged, and she became the First Lady of the Jacob's Ladder Family, the Women's Ministry Director, the Church Executive Administrator and the Dean of the California University of Theology. Dr. Robert and Paulette Douglas are the proud parents of three wonderful children, Shakinah, Robert Jr. and Sondra Imani. They are also blessed with two granddaughters, Demi and Rob'Ann (butter ball) four grandsons, Dylan, Dominick Terrell, the twins Canden and Caden. Seven Godchildren and twelve God -grandchildren. Dr. Douglas is a graduate from Fuller Theological Seminary, Pasadena, California, Pentecostal Bible College, Ministerial Training Institute of Inglewood, California and Aenon Bible College West Coast. She has a Bachelors degree in Biblical Studies, a Masters degree in Theology, a PhD in Theology, Administration and a PhD in Biblical Counseling. She has earned certificates from California Christian Leadership of Orange County in biblical counseling, Zoe Christian Leadership Training Institute, Church Growth International, Seoul Korea and School of World Missions and Evangelism, Los Angeles. Dr. Douglas is formerly the Dean/Professor of the Inglewood Ministerial Training Institute of Inglewood, the Inland Empire Ministerial Training Institute, the Tri-County Ministerial Training Institute (San Bernardino, Riverside and Los Angeles counties) and the Living Waters Bible College, Rialto California. Dr. Douglas is presently the Dean of Colleges and Professor for the California District Council Aenon Bible College and Institutes, the Jacob's Ladder California University of Theology and Aenon Bible Institute CDC Extension Campus in Inglewood, California and the American College Theological Seminary International University (ACTS). All schools are fully accredited institutions for pastors, evangelist, teachers and anyone who has the call of God on their lives for ministry. Dr. Douglas is currently the CDC International Missions President and the past Church/Extension/Evangelism/Altar Director for the California District Council of the Pentecostal Assemblies of the World, Inc. Past Evangelism President for the CHDC Area 2 and has worked with the PAW Evangelism Ministry for more than 35 years. Dr. Paulette Douglas is the published author of the book series "Get Rid of It before It Gets Rid of You". Self-Help Instructions on how to correct and receive deliverance in every area of your life. Dr. Douglas portrays tremendous strength and endurance in the Lord by jointly sharing the vision and love for God with Bishop Douglas. Her primary objective in life is to be that "Excellent Woman of God, walking in His Divine favor.

Books and Recourses Compiled by
Dr. Paulette Douglas

"How to Get Rid of "it", Before "it" Gets Rid of You" Series (12 Books on Self Deliverance)

Volume One- Healing and Deliverance from Additions

Volume Two- Healing and Deliverance from Sexual Additions

Volume Three- Healing and Deliverance from Personality Disorders

Volume Four- Healing and Deliverance from Negative Relationships

Volume Five- Healing and Deliverance Through Spiritual Warfare

Volume Six- Healing and Deliverance from Negatives Attitudes

Volume Seven- Healing and Deliverance from Success Hindrances

Volume Eight- Healing and Deliverance from Tormenting Emotions

Volume Nine- Healing and Deliverance from Spiritual Weakness

Volume Ten- Healing and Deliverance from Salvation Issues

Volume Eleven- Healing and Deliverance from Domestic Problems

Volume Twelve- Healing and Deliverance Through Biblical Counseling

How to Have an Anointed Altar Workers Ministry

How to Have an Effective Prayer and Fasting Life

How to Walk in Your Grace as the Wife of a Minister, Deacon, Pastor, or Bishop

How to be an Effective Life Coach

www.ingramcontent.com/pod-product-compliance
Lightning Source LLC
Chambersburg PA
CBHW08184525026
48659CB00008B/2616